PENGUIN BOOKS

JOURNEY AROUND MY ROOM

Louise Bogan, the author of six books of poetry—one of which won the Bollingen Prize—three books of criticism, five translations, and one anthology for children, was Consultant in Poetry to the Library of Congress from 1945 to 1946 and poetry critic for *The New Yorker* from 1931 to 1969. She died in 1970.

Ruth Limmer, a former editor and professor of English at the Western College for Women in Oxford, Ohio, now works as a program planner for the National Endowment for the Arts. She has edited a collection of the letters of Louise Bogan, *What the Woman Lived,* and collaborated with Robert Phelps on a volume of Louise Bogan's collected criticism, *A Poet's Alphabet.*

BOOKS BY LOUISE BOGAN

POETRY

Body of This Death / 1923
Dark Summer / 1929
The Sleeping Fury / 1937
Poems and New Poems / 1941
Collected Poems 1923–1953 / 1954
The Blue Estuaries: Poems 1923–1968 / 1968

CRITICISM

Achievement in American Poetry, 1900–1950 / 1951
Selected Criticism: Poetry and Prose / 1955
A Poet's Alphabet: Reflection on the
    Literary Art and Vocation / 1970

LETTERS

What the Woman Lived / 1973

TRANSLATIONS

With Elizabeth Mayer
The Glass Bees *by Ernst Juenger* / 1960
Elective Affinities *by Goethe* / 1963
The Sorrows of Young Werther *and* Novella
    by Goethe / 1971
With Elizabeth Roget
The Journal of Jules Renard / 1964

ANTHOLOGY

With William Jay Smith
The Golden Journey: Poems for Young People / 1965

Journey Around My Room

The Autobiography of
Louise Bogan

ɛ ɛ

A Mosaic by Ruth Limmer

PENGUIN BOOKS

Penguin Books Ltd, Harmondsworth,
Middlesex, England
Penguin Books, 625 Madison Avenue,
New York, New York 10022, U.S.A.
Penguin Books Australia Ltd, Ringwood,
Victoria, Australia
Penguin Books Canada Limited, 2801 John Street,
Markham, Ontario, Canada L3R 1B4
Penguin Books (N.Z.) Ltd, 182–190 Wairau Road,
Auckland 10, New Zealand

First published in the United States of America by
The Viking Press 1980
Published in Penguin Books 1981

LIBRARY OF CONGRESS CATALOGING IN PUBLICATION DATA
Bogan, Louise, 1897–1970.
Journey around my room.
1. Bogan, Louise, 1897–1970—Biography.
2. Authors, American—20th century—Biography.
I. Limmer, Ruth. II. Title.
PS3503.O195Z464   1981   811'.52   [B]   81-10573
ISBN 0 14 00.5923 7   AACR2

Printed in the United States of America by
Offset Paperback Mfrs., Inc., Dallas, Pennsylvania
Set in Linotype Fairfield

TRAIN TUNE

Back through clouds
Back through clearing
Back through distance
Back through silence

Back through groves
Back through garlands
Back by rivers
Back below mountains

Back through lightning
Back through cities
Back through stars
Back through hours

Back through plains
Back through flowers
Back through birds
Back through rain

Back through smoke
Back through noon
Back along love
Back through midnight

ACKNOWLEDGMENTS

To Amanda Vaill, who conceived the idea, and to the others who eased its birth: Marshall Clement and David Stivender, who together elegantly simplified the task of locating LB's uncollected prose and poetry; J. Richard Philips, who secured the Bogan Papers for the Amherst College Library; Darlene Holdsworth, whose archivist talents made my search through those papers so easy a task; and John Lancaster, present curator of rare books at the Amherst Library, whose courtesies were unfailing. I am grateful to them and to Glyn Morris, Patricia Willis, curator of the Marianne Moore Archive at the Rosenbach Foundation, and especially Mildred Weston, for making new caches of letters from LB available to me. For the remarkable family snapshots, none ever before published, as well as for all but one of the later photographs, I am deeply, and joyfully, indebted to Maidie Alexander Scannell, LB's "daughter and friend."

Contents

Introduction

๕ ๕ There exists a somewhat disconcerting photograph of Louise Bogan, taken in her sixties during one of her stays at the MacDowell Colony, which shows her seated at a table, seemingly about to speak. The studio in which she sits is spacious and quiet, and although from the angle from which it is photographed, we can see no pictures on the wall, it might otherwise have been furnished for her. To her left is a piano and an open casement window facing the woods. Before her, on the table, a book and a pile of neatly stacked paper; under her large hands, which brace a pencil, a pad of lined yellow paper. She is conservatively dressed: flowered blouse and a raspberry-colored cable-stitched cardigan. Around her fine dark hair, to keep it from drifting, is an inch-wide band of black ribbon. At her throat, a silver clip of some sort. A seashell? She wears, that we can see, a smallish round earring with a fleur-de-lis incised in its center.

But her expression is less than serene. Viewed from a distance, her great gray eyes appear startled, almost glaring, as if she were about to protest an interruption. In that instant, the visitor might well back away, intimidated. Close up, however, the picture changes: the eyes soften; they are amused. The half-open mouth under the long Irish lip is moving into a smile. In the multiple reading it projects—close and far—the photograph captures a truth: at a distance Louise Bogan was often formidable. Reserved, dignified, gracious but capable of withering sharpness, the woman in the picture is the author of the Bogan oeuvre: pure formal poetry and elegant, authoritative criticism, both of astonishing beauty. But she is not someone who will curl up familiarly with the reader and share personal anecdotes in a review, nor will she litter her poems with autobiographical details.

The Bogan who speaks in this book is also reserved, also dignified, but here she tells us what it is like to *be* the woman who produced the oeuvre. To be moved by this voice requires no knowledge of Bogan as critic or poet. The reader needs only to listen attentively, as to a seashell, from which comes a sound that, in her own haunting phrase, "will chime you change and hours."

Yet precisely because she chose privacy, many readers have been avid to learn the circumstances of her life. These are supplied in the chronology beginning on page xxv. For those meeting her for the first time, however, perhaps it is enough to say that Louise Bogan was a New Englander by birth and accent, and a New Yorker by choice. She was a woman of letters in much the way that her friend Edmund Wilson was a man of letters: all her activities centered on literature—creating it, appraising it, explaining it, championing it. But unlike Wilson, she never became widely known, perhaps because she deplored the uses of publicity, perhaps because she was too austere, perhaps because she was a woman in a man's world, perhaps because in a political age she abhorred politics of all kinds and chose not to exercise the authority that was hers.

However one accounts for it, Bogan, largely unknown to the public but esteemed by her peers, chose for over thirty years to live anonymously in what she described as a *faubourg*—Washington Heights, on northern Manhattan Island, where her life could be her own.

As she explained in 1940 to Mildred Weston, an acquaintance from Spokane with whom she corresponded over many years:

> I have very few of the usual warm friendships that normal people have, and enjoy. I do not want to make myself out a kind of monster, but it is a sad fact that it is now easier for me to think of a person I admire and like, saying Well, she (or he) is *there*, and exists—and to say and think this with pleasure, than it is to do anything about it.

While this apologia appears to underestimate how much she actually gave of herself, it is essentially descriptive. Bogan made friends easily—her ability to charm birds off trees would have endangered all the flocks of North America had she chosen to exercise it frequently—but she was nevertheless deeply reserved: highly suspicious of people who might want to use her and necessarily protective of her gifts and energy. Very early on, she wrote in a poem called "Fifteenth Farewell": ". . . The slight life in my throat will not give pause /

For your love, nor your loss, nor any cause." Nor would it in later years. She came first.

A poet friend who came to understand her position fondly described one of her less convincing dodges. In *Louise Bogan: A Woman's Words*, her sometime collaborator William Jay Smith wrote that for many years when he called, hoping to meet her for lunch, she would explain that she couldn't that day: she was going to the dentist. After a time, he realized that no one could so regularly and inconveniently have dental appointments. She simply did not choose to see him, or anyone, that day.

But even limited access held great rewards. As the novelist and editor William Maxwell wrote in *The New Yorker*'s obituary: "One look at her work—or sometimes one look at her—made any number of disheartened artists take heart and go on being the kind of dedicated creature they were intended to be."

A person with such well-built defenses against sharing herself is unlikely to write an autobiography. And she didn't. Indeed, she is unlikely to make known even the basic facts that appear in biographical compendia. In 1939, asked to supply information for a standard if rather chatty research volume, she produced (but finally didn't send) the following excursion into sarcasm:

> My dislike of telling future research students anything about myself is intense and profound. If they know everything to begin with, how in hell can they go on eating up their tidy little fellowships researching? And I believe the less authentic records are, the more "interesting" they automatically become. Then, too, of course, I have many dark deeds in my past which I shall have to cover up, for posterity's sake. I remember very well, at the age of seven or so, making away with

a couple of little gold baby-pins, fastened with a chain, a contraption which fascinated me, from the top of a bureau belonging to a girl with long curls, who was older than I was, called Ethel Gardener, in Ballardville, Massachusetts. I also have liked throwing things away and hiding them, ever since I can remember. I poked a small ring, decorated with a red stone resembling a ruby, down a crack in a staircase, in Bodwell's Hotel, in Milton, New Hampshire, around 1901, and I always used to bury my rag doll, Mag, and dig her up again. In the convent I fell in love with an altar boy, and wrote him a passionate letter, which was later found by a nun, and almost resulted in my getting expelled, then and there. Nothing came of this however, and I won a book, that year, for Catechism, and the Gold Cross for General Excellence, the next. (This cross was later pawned by my unfortunate brother, so I can't send it to you to prove my story.)

So you can see, it is just as well if I don't delve into my past. I used to lie in confession regularly, I must warn you, from the time I first confessed, at the ripe moral age of about nine, through a harp draped with a dust-cover, in the convent parlor. (They must have been varnishing the confessionals.)

My great gifts of imagination always took the form of lies, in fact, up to my entrance into puberty, when I became a radical and a Fabian, and discovered Bernard Shaw, Aubrey Beardsley, Arthur Symons, Nietzsche, Wagner, Max Stirner and Walter Pater. My first literary exercises were strongly influenced by William Morris and D. G. Rossetti and I wrote a long poem, or a sonnet sequence, every day, for about four years, after coming home from school. The effect of these labors, after about two years, was that I got conditioned, one June, in Greek, Latin, French, algebra—in everything, in fact, but English Composition. I was always rather good in physics and geometry, although my struggles, in the laboratory, with Bunsen burners and Gilley boilers would have made the hair rise on the head of any competent physicist. —I used to weep, when under the influence of other people's poetry, and have a rush of blood to the head, resulting in violent nose-running and sneezes, when the muse descended on *me*. (This symptom passed, after about eighteen, and I don't suppose I have ever been authentically visited by Apollo, since.) I used to get very sick to my stomach in public, too, around this time.

My passage from puberty into early maturity was swift, and I prefer to draw the veil over my experiences, sexual and otherwise, from the age of nineteen, when I married for the first time, to the present. I think the researchers of the future should have a little spice to help them on their way, and if they succeed in discovering any of my adventures, in detail, during this period (as I doubt that they can, since except for ten years passed among the so-called bourgeoisie, my life at this time was lived among the lower-middle class, and they have short memories, owing to defective intellects and short memory spans). That I have no criminal records is entirely due to the kindness of several members of the legal and psychiatric professions, who, I am sure, put me down as nuts, and just let me go on thinking that a stay in the booby-hatch, now and again, would not run into as much money as a stay in jail.

Well, where were we? O yes. —In regard to your detailed questions, may I reply as follows, taking them up seriatim, as the saying goes.

Birthplace: Livermore Falls, Maine, a town on the Androscoggin River, run by a paper mill. My father has often told me about the excellent hard cider made by Billy Bean, the proprietor of the town's combination brothel and saloon. B. Bean used to add all sorts of things to the original apple juice, including ground up sirloin steak, and the results of drinking this nectar, when it was ripe, were terrific. I often like to think that I bear traces of this fire-water in the ichor which runs in my own veins. . . .

Influences: I think alcohol comes in here. I began to drink

steadily after meeting one Raymond Holden, although I had been known to crook my arm, on two continents, before that. I like Mai-bowle with wild-strawberries in it, champagne, rye, and anything which happens to stay in a bottle, best.

Development: Slow and unsteady.

Political convictions: NONE.

Likes and dislikes: My God: what do you think this is: an encyclopedia? —I love food, music, beautiful and *beau/belle-laid(e)* people of both sexes, babes in arms, flowers, clean rooms, aired sheets, oil-lamps, and books about bad taste. I also like love-making, when it is really well-informed, and some varieties of landscape. I dislike swimming, bathing in lakes or the sea, horse-back riding, and dirty fingernails. Also: well-bred accents, loud talk, the professional literati of all ages, other women poets (jealousy!), other men poets, English accents, Yale graduates and bad writing and bad writers.

She goes on in this vein, not answering questions about dates, parentage, education, beginnings of career, favorite authors (among whom "also Mallarmé and Yeats and whoever wrote 'Johnny I hardly knew yeh' . . .") until she winds up, sincerely, Louise Marie Beatrice Bogan.

So much for the serious researcher. Yet this book *is* autobiography. It is the autobiography of a writer who could say, in speaking of her poetry, "I have written down my experience in the closest detail. But the rough and vulgar facts are not there." Not there, and essentially not anywhere, except for journal entries spreading across a couple of months in 1933, when a few raw facts erupt at a time of humiliation and pain. Their presence disturbs the temperature of the narrative, but not, I think, to its disadvantage. It is almost a relief to see flames when everywhere one feels heat. And how extraordinary, for once, to see behind some of the poems to the situations that gave them birth. Which is not to say that the facts explain the poems. Quite the contrary. The poems, the stories, the crafted prose that compose the narrative are the truths the facts direct us toward.

Thus, Chapter 8, composed of poems written and published during the first decade of her professional career, and then rejected totally, will tell us nothing about whom she saw and what she did during that period. But interspersed as it is with remarks about poetry, the chapter reveals a great deal about Bogan, the self-censoring conscious artist. Given her particular nature, attending to these remarkable castoffs is as instructive as an account of the life itself. The voyeur in us might prefer another form of revelation: details about her early bohemianism, for example, but she doesn't supply them. Austerity interposes.

The frame of the autobiography is a story Louise Bogan wrote for *The New Yorker* in 1933, called "Journey Around My Room," a meditation inspired by *Voyage autour de ma chambre* by the eighteenth-century Frenchman Xavier de Maistre. Bogan's own "journey," set here in italics, opens and closes the book, and is otherwise used to begin certain chapters. At the age of thirty-six she had already set the exploratory tone: "How did I get here, below this ceiling, above this floor?" The remainder of the autobiography, continuing to explore, is composed of journals, notebook entries, poems (some never before published), sentences and paragraphs from her criticism, portions of letters, a lecture, answers to questions (in one case, questions she herself posed), short stories, recorded conversations, scraps of paper. . . .

As arranged, the selections develop a roughly chronological

autobiography. But the chronology is tempered by the nature of the material. Traditionally, the writer of autobiography views his or her life from a single piece of high ground, reached after arduous climbing. From that vantage point, the writer looks down and back, drawing the territory of the past as he sees it in the present. Some of the mapping in this book happens exactly that way, but in other cases the record is simultaneous with the experience, or only slightly later. In still other cases, we get reflections written at various times, over decades, and for various purposes. The effect should be no more unsettling than an artist's retrospective, so hung that it is chronological over all, but for effect the self-portraits—in pastels, oils, and pen and ink, and done over four decades— are grouped together.

The autobiographical account is far from complete. To begin with, few of her personal papers survived a fire in late December 1929. One diary that did come through unscathed relates to her time in Europe in 1922. As she tells us on p. 161, understating the case, it lacks descriptive power. We learn that she heard Mahler's Second Symphony, that she ate eggs for lunch, danced, went to Thomas Cook for her mail . . . but the entries sit on the page, lifeless and unpublishable. For another, she was neither a diary nor a journal keeper. Years go by without a paragraph, or with only literary entries—quotations from books read—to fill up a half dozen pages of the school notebooks she was fond of using.

From what remains, it is clear that Bogan's childhood, about which she wrote in her thirties and again, with greater depth and poignancy, during her fifties and sixties, was a key to the person she became. It is less clear that other periods, about which she remains silent, or almost so, were not equally, if differently, significant. Most of these periods can never be re-

covered as she viewed them. All the editor can do, to bridge
the lacunae, is to arrange the available material in such a way
as to suggest the flow of experience. As for events, the stuff
of traditional autobiography, they will rarely appear.

Thus, she will write nothing about her first marriage, at the
age of nineteen, to a corporal (later a lieutenant and a captain)
in the American Army. Her mother was opposed, she told
me once; she threatened, had a heart attack. "But I was trying
to escape." Instead of going on to Radcliffe, where she had
been offered a scholarship after one year at Boston University,
she defied her mother and married. The next year, four months
pregnant, she followed her husband to the Canal Zone. "It was
the only time in my life I was seasick. They took me off
the boat on a stretcher" and set her down in a "concrete
Government flat in the wilds of Panama." It was an alien
and hostile landscape as seen by the young New Englander,
the youth from "a land of change." More distressing than the
landscape was that "All we had in common was sex. Nothing
to talk about. We played *cards*," she said. "I left him and went
home to Boston with the fat baby in my arms. He came after
me four [?] months later, and we moved to an island off
Portland. Then the war was over and we went to Hoboken.
Curt was a paper man, involved in discharging the soldiers.
That's when—from Hoboken—I began meeting some of the
Greenwich Village group. I was learning to become us. I
was becoming us. . . . After a while, I gathered the baby in
my arms and left him for good. What could I do. One must
break free. One must burst forth."

Never again did she refer to the subject, except to say,
later in the conversation, that Curt Alexander had died in
1920. Two identifiable poems remain from the Canal Zone
period: "A Tale" opens her first volume of poetry, *Body of*

This Death, as it opens her last volume, *The Blue Estuaries.* "Decoration" followed immediately upon "A Tale" in the first volume and never appeared again, except in Louis Untermeyer's anthology *Modern American Poetry,* where he included it in edition after edition and made her furious. If she had dropped it, so should he.

Among the other things she will not tell us here is that she clerked in Brentano's bookstore and worked briefly as an assistant in branches of the New York Public Library (Marianne Moore worked in one of them also but Bogan was too shy to introduce herself and Miss Moore was too abstracted to notice). She also filed cards in the office of Columbia University's distinguished sociologist William Fielding Ogburn, a job found for her by a fellow poet, Margaret Mead.

She'll not tell us that when she went abroad in 1922, on her tiny widow's pension, to study piano in Vienna, she lived on the Berggasse, Freud's street. Nor will she mention that before she left, Harriet Monroe wrote that five of her poems, under the collective title "Beginning and End," had been accepted by *Poetry* magazine. The following year, when her first collection of poetry was published, she exhibited the already severe standards she set for herself by excluding from that volume four of the five poems Miss Monroe had printed.

She will not say that her long career as a critic began in 1924 with a review of D. H. Lawrence's *Birds, Beasts, and Flowers* for the *New Republic,* or that in the year before she had fallen in love with Raymond Holden, who was to become her second husband. ("People used to say I taught him how to write, but that's nonsense. He had a lovely lyric gift; he wrote charming things when he was young.")

There is a great deal more she will not say. The fact of the matter is that Bogan was far more absorbed by the texture and meaning of experience than with the events giving rise to them. Readers seeking the array of anecdote and the kind of factual detail we have come to expect from autobiography will not find them here. In their place, we have the point and purpose of the writer's life—the work itself.

Nevertheless, *Journey Around My Room* is surely not the autobiography Louise Bogan would have written had she chosen to. A stage manager, not the playwright, has decided on the scenes and acts and on how to arrange and light the script. These are not her choices of prose or poetry, not her sequences, not her chapter divisions. But the book *always* speaks in her voice and is true to her experience as she revealed it. If distortion there is, it lies in the relative absence of humor. With her high Irish wit—that sometimes, it must be confessed, drew blood—Louise Bogan was one of the most amusing people of her time. To be with her was to laugh with her, and perhaps her highest accolade was, "We laugh in the same places." Only a few days before her sudden death on February 4, 1970, from a coronary occlusion,[*] hilariously embroidering over the telephone on the theme of God and His intentions for the lowly groundhog, she said proudly but a little sadly, "Well, at least I can still make people laugh." If she had written a formal autobiography, there would, I expect, have been great runs of laughter, exuberance, and joy. That there are relatively few here is another reason to rage at the injustices and brevity of life. Happily, art is long.

---

[*] In her chapter on Louise Bogan in *A World of Light*, May Sarton suggests that the cause of death was misstated in *What the Woman Lived*, Bogan's selected letters, and implies that there may have been good reason to obscure the truth. "Coronary occlusion" was determined by the medical examiner. Those closest to her, including her daughter, had and have no reason whatever to contemplate, or to hide, another cause.

Chronology

      This chronology makes no attempt to list all of LB's published writings. It does account for every book and introduction, and it gives publication dates for some of her earliest poetry. It attempts, but largely fails, to account for all the places she lived (where no city is indicated, the location is always New York City) and, with more success, to date milestones.

1897   11 August, born, to Mary (Murphy) Shields and Daniel J. Bogan, in Livermore Falls, Maine. (Their first child, her brother Charles, was born in 1885.)

1901   Milton, New Hampshire

1904 Ballardvale, Massachusetts

1906–7 Year of schooling at Mount St. Mary's Convent in Manchester, New Hampshire, while her mother is on a trip that takes her as far as California

1909 March, family moves to Boston

1910 Enters Girls' Latin School, where her poems will be printed in the school magazine

1915 September, enters as a freshman at Boston University. Two poems of hers will be printed in the Boston University *Beacon*.

1916 Marries Curt Alexander, a professional Army man, and for at least part of the year they live in New York, on Bleecker Street

1917 May, goes to the Panama Canal Zone, where Alexander is stationed
19 October, gives birth to a daughter
December, first professional publication, in *Others*, of two poems, "Betrothed" and "The Young Wife"

1918 May, returns alone to Boston with baby
October, brother, serving in France in World War I, dies in battle
Moves with husband to an Army base on an island off Portland, Maine

1919 With husband, moves to Garden Street in Hoboken, New Jersey
Separates from husband for second, and final, time

1920 Lives variously in New York City, where she clerks

in Brentano's bookstore, and Farley, Massachusetts

Husband dies at age 32

1921   Lives in New York City and, at least occasionally, in Worcester, Massachusetts

July, Harriet Monroe accepts five poems for *Poetry* (published August 1922)

1922   January, begins work at various branches (Hudson Park, Woodstock, Tompkins Square) of the New York Public Library

15 April, on SS *Homeric*, starts "sabbatical six months" in Vienna, where she studies piano; returns 26 September

1923   *Body of This Death*, dedicated to her mother and daughter, published by Robert McBride & Co.

Begins association with Raymond Holden

1924   Lives variously at 99 Henry Street, Brooklyn; Otter River, Massachusetts; and 242 Lexington Avenue

March, first review: D. H. Lawrence's *Birds, Beasts, and Flowers,* for *New Republic*

Catalogues for sociologist at Columbia University

November, accepts managing editorship of *The Measure* ("I'll accept anything to bolster me out of all this lares and penates.")

1925   Moves, with Raymond Holden, to 93 Cedar Street ("over against the Charles Street jail"), Boston

July, marries Holden

August, they move to 66 Fayette Street, Boston

1926   August, spends month at Yaddo, the literary colony

that opens this year ("I have done two stories and two poems, since I came. Curiously enough, the place does make you feel like working.")

December, they move to Santa Fe, New Mexico, for Holden's health

1927   May, they return to New York ("I could live behind a billboard or on a roof, to be back among people I know.")

October, writes film criticism for *New Republic*

1928   Moves with Holden to Hillsdale (Columbia County), New York

1929   *Dark Summer*, dedicated to Raymond Holden, published by Charles Scribner's Sons

26 December, house in Hillsdale burns down ("All our things went too—books, pictures, and almost all our manuscripts.")

1930   Moves with Holden to 5 Prospect Place (Tudor City in Manhattan)

Receives John Reed Memorial Prize, *Poetry* ("That the prize was given to my work in general delights me, because I have never been able to compete, in contests, or to write to order or on terms.")

1931   21 March, first review written for *The New Yorker* is published

April, enters New York Neurological Institute ("I refused to fall apart, so I have been taken apart, like a watch.")

May, recuperates at Cromwell Sanitarium in Connecticut

June, returns to 5 Prospect Place

October, she and Holden move to 306 Lexington Avenue

1933   Awarded a Guggenheim Fellowship for creative writing abroad

April, leaves for Italy

June, south of France; stays briefly with Ford Madox Ford and Janice Biala; thence to Toulon and Salzburg

November, second breakdown, enters the New York Hospital's Westchester Division, "Bloomingdale's" in White Plains, New York ("I have every confidence in this place and plan to stay here until I'm good and cured.")

1934   March, discusses with her editor at Scribner's the possibility of a book to be called *Laura Dailey's Story* (". . . the thing should be a 'play of sensibility' over the mill-towns of my childhood.")

May, living at 100 West 55th Street

Separates from Holden

October, moves to 82 Washington Place

1935   Begins relationship with Theodore Roethke ("I hope that one or two immortal lyrics will come out of all this tumbling about.")

September, evicted from Washington Place apartment and moves to Hotel Albert on University Place ("I've had a sort of mild illumination about how important money is, since I saw the sheriff standing on my floor, and saw the furniture whisked out the door onto the sidewalk.")

1936   May, living at 70 Morningside Drive

Summer, trip to Quebec and to Swampscott, Massachusetts. She will return to Swampscott, to stay at the Willey House, almost every year from now on.

September, moves to 302 West 77th Street

26 December, mother dies at age 72 ("—In death she looks terribly scornful and proud, but I think she loved up to the end.")

1937 *The Sleeping Fury*, dedicated to Edmund Wilson, published by Scribner's

Awarded Helen Haire Levinson Prize, *Poetry*

February, divorce from Holden becomes final

April, takes up unexpired term of Guggenheim Fellowship and visits Ireland

Begins "successful love-affair" with man she meets on shipboard. It lasts until 1945. (". . . perfect freedom, perfect detachment, *no jealousy* at all—an emphasis on *joy*.")

July, moves to 709 West 169th Street, where she maintains an apartment for the rest of her life

1939 Participates in *Partisan Review* symposium on "The Situation in American Writing." (She describes her contribution as "my *coeur mis à nu*" and says, "I certainly would not have opened up like this a few years ago. . . . And I really think it is a little *vulgar*, to do it now. But what the hell. . . .")

1941 *Poems and New Poems*, published by Scribner's

1943 Breaks with Scribner's

1944 Gives Hopwood Lecture, University of Michigan

Begins judging applications for Guggenheim Fellowships in poetry, which she will continue into the 1960s

November, elected Fellow in American Letters of the Library of Congress ("For many years I have thought that my value as a writer consisted, in some part, in my separation from most of the activities of 'the literary scene.' This separation I never wanted to become rigid; and during the last year I have found a more flexible attitude a natural thing: part of a process of growth.")

1945   Takes up appointment as Consultant in Poetry to the Library of Congress and is lent an apartment in Georgetown at 1207 35th Street, N.W., Washington, D.C.

1946   August, term as Consultant ends; returns to New York

Serves as consultant on belles-lettres to Doubleday (to 1947)

1948   Wins Harriet Monroe Award, University of Chicago

Spends part of summer in Seattle, teaching at the University of Washington at Roethke's recommendation

Again considers writing "stories" about her childhood

November, with T. S. Eliot and other Fellows in American Letters, awards the first Bollingen Prize to Ezra Pound

1949   Winter term, visiting lecturer in humanities at University of Chicago

Translates Goethe's *Elective Affinities* with Elizabeth Mayer (not published until 1963)

1950   June–July, travels to West Coast, returns via Utah
       and Indiana, where she reads and lectures at uni-
       versities, an activity she will continue into the 1960s
       Bibliography compiled while Consultant in Poetry—
       *Works in the Humanities Published in Great Britain
       1939–46*—published by Library of Congress
       August, begins *Achievement in American Poetry,
       1900–1950*

1951   *Achievement* published
       Receives $1000 grant from National Institute of Arts
       and Letters
       Introduction to Harper's Modern Classics edition of
       W. H. Hudson's *Green Mansions*
       December, father dies at age 90

1952   Elected to membership in Institute of Arts and Letters
       Spring, visiting professor at University of Arkansas

1953   April–May in England

1954   Writes on current situation in American poetry for
       Times (London) *Literary Supplement*
       Begins teaching evening class in poetry at New York
       University, which she continues into the 1960s
       Collected Poems 1923–1953

1955   Receives Bollingen Prize, shared with Léonie Adams
       November, reads at West Coast colleges
       Selected Criticism: Poetry and Prose, dedicated to
       "Maidie Alexander, daughter and friend"

1956   February, gives Bergen Lecture at Yale
       June, receives honorary degree from The Western

College for Women, Oxford, Ohio ("I hereby promise not to go around calling myself *Dr.* Bogan.")

Autumn, begins teaching course in poetry at YMHA
in New York City (Marianne Moore is enrolled.
"How thrilling!")

1957   First brief stay at MacDowell Colony. She will go
there with some regularity from now on. ("I shall be
sixty in August, and it is time for me to investigate
colonies. Up to this time I have been too *young* to
think of them!")

1958   Summer, lectures at the Salzburg Seminar in American Studies; then visits Switzerland, Paris, and London

Introduction to New Directions edition of Flaubert's
Sentimental Education

Provides critical notes to translation of Iwan Goll's
Jean sans terre

1959   Receives $5000 award from Academy of American
Poets ("I shall plan to use the cash for pleasure and
relaxation—for time spent by the sea and in the
mountains. The honor will bolster me in doubtful
times.")

Translations, with May Sarton, of seven poems by
Paul Valéry, four published in *Hudson Review,*
three in *Poetry*

October, delivers a paper on Emily Dickinson as part
of the bicentennial celebration of the town of Amherst, Massachusetts

1960   Spring, visiting professor at University of Washington
while Roethke is on leave

June, honorary degree from Colby College, Maine
Foreword to Hawthorne's *The Scarlet Letter*
Translation, with Elizabeth Mayer, of Ernst Juenger's *The Glass Bees*

1961 Writes long essay, "A Lifework," on Robert Frost for *Major Writers of America*

1962 March, receives Senior Creative Arts Award from Brandeis University ("I am v. much touched, of course, since it is the first recognition ever to come to me from the good old Bay State.")
  October, gives lecture, "What the Women Said," at Bennington College; participates—reading, and paper on "The Role of the Poetry Journal"—in the National Poetry Festival held at the Library of Congress

1963 April–June in England

1964 February, only winter stay at MacDowell Colony
  September, returns to Boston area (16 Chauncey Street, Cambridge) to begin year as visiting professor at Brandeis University
  Translation, with Elizabeth Roget, of *The Journal of Jules Renard*

1965 June, after teaching stint at Brandeis, re-enters Neurological Institute, a few doors down from her home on 169th Street, suffering from depression
  September–December, at Bloomingdale Hospital, White Plains, New York
  The Golden Journey, an anthology of poems for young people, with William Jay Smith ("We did

it . . . practically by reciting the stuff to each other *out loud!*")

1966   Introduction to *A Cookbook for Poor Poets and Others* by Ann Rogers ("Poets are often out of funds. Many times they try to keep body and soul together by eating candy bars, apples, doughnuts, and an occasional hamburger, usually standing up. This is a mistake. Meals should be eaten sitting down.")

1967   February, reads and teaches at the Poetry Center of the University of Arizona
       August–October, England and Scotland
       Receives $10,000 National Endowment for the Arts Award
       November, first overt political activity: to protest the war in Vietnam, she reads at Poets for Peace rally in Town Hall

1968   Collaborates with Josephine O'Brien Schaefer on "afterword" to New American Library edition of V. Woolf's *A Writer's Diary* ("I am so tired of people mooning over her. She had a v. inhuman side.")

1969   January, flies, for the first time, to take up one-month appointment as poet-in-residence at Hollins College, Virginia
       March, *The Blue Estuaries: Poems 1923–1968*, dedicated "To the memory of my father, mother and brother"
       May, elected to the American Academy of Arts and Letters
       October, resigns, after 38 years, as poetry reviewer of *The New Yorker* ("Remember, this takes *courage.*")

November, a "reading-chat" on poetry for children, with William Cole and Padraic Colum, at Library of Congress

Samuel Barber's setting of her "To Be Sung on the Water" published by Schirmer

1970   4 February, dies alone in her apartment on 169th Street

A Poet's Alphabet: Reflections on the Literary Art and Vocation published posthumously. ("I *do* want to see it! If all that work had gone down the (journalist) drain, it would have been sad. As it is, I can *crow* a little!")

1971   Earlier translation, with Elizabeth Mayer, of Goethe's *The Sorrows of Young Werther* and *Novella* published with an introduction by W. H. Auden

Journey
Around
My Room

1 Back through clouds

❦ ❦ The most advantageous point from which to start this journey is the bed itself, wherein, at midnight or early in the morning, the adventurous traveller lies moored, the terrain spread out before him. The most fortunate weather is warm to cool, engendered by a westerly breeze, borne from the open window toward the ashes in the grate. At midnight, moonlight lies upon the floor, to guide the traveller's eye; in the early morning, the bleak opacity that serves the traveller in this region as sun brightens the brick wall of the house across the yard, and sheds a feeble reflected glow upon all the objects which I shall presently name.

This is a largish room, almost square in shape. It faces east and west, and is bounded on the north by the hall, which leads, after some hesitation, to the kitchen; on the south by someone's bedroom in the house next door; on the west, by backyards and the Empire State Building; on the east, by Lexington Avenue, up and down which electric cars roll with a noise like water running into a bottle. Its four walls are chastely papered with Manila paper. Its floor is inadequately varnished. Its ceiling bears all the honors away: it is quite lofty in pitch, and it is clean, absolutely unspotted, in fact, save for a little damp over the fireplace, which, from some angles, looks like a fish. A fireplace, resembling a small black arch, occupies a middle position in the south wall. Above it, a plain deal mantelpiece of ordinary design supports a row of books, a photograph of the News Building taken from the Chanin Building, four shells from a Maine beach, and a tin of Famous Cake Box Mixture. Above these objects hangs a Japanese print, depicting Russian sailors afflicted by an angry ocean, searchlights, a burning ship, and a boatload of raging Japanese.

The initial mystery that attends any journey is: how did the traveller reach his starting point in the first place? How did I reach the window, the walls, the fireplace, the room itself; how do I happen to be beneath this ceiling and above this floor? Oh, that is a matter for conjecture, for argument pro and con, for research, supposition, dialectic! I can hardly remember how. Unlike Livingstone, on the verge of darkest Africa, I have no maps to hand, no globe of the terrestrial or the celestial spheres, no chart of mountains, lakes, no sextant, no artificial horizon. If ever I possessed a compass, it has long since disappeared. There must be, however, some reasonable explanation for my presence here. Some step started me to-

ward this point, as opposed to all other points on the habitable globe. I must consider; I must discover it.

And here it is. One morning in March, in the year 1909, my father opened the storm door leading from the kitchen to the backsteps, on Chestnut Street, in Ballardvale, a small town in Massachusetts, on the Boston & Maine Railroad. . . .

Although the houses stood securely fastened to the ground, as always, everything in the town went wild in autumn and blew about the streets. Smoke blew wildly from chimneys and torrents of leaves were pulled from the trees; they rushed across the sidewalks and blew against wagons and people and trains; they blew uphill and fell from great heights and small ones; they fell to the ground and into the river. Clouds rode high in the sky; the sun shone brilliantly everywhere. Or else half the town would lie in the shadow of a long cloud and half the town would stand shining bright, the weather-vanes almost as still in a strong blast coming from one quarter as in no wind at all, the paint sparkling on the clapboards. Sometimes in the late afternoon the full sun came from two directions at once, from the west and reflected in a full blaze from the windows of houses looking westward.

The children were blown home from school, shouting and running, along with the leaves. They were blown up paths to side doors, or through orchards, or into back yards, where perhaps their mothers stood, taking the last clothes in off the line, apron strings flying out from their waists. The children rushed into kitchens that smelled of baking or of ironed clothes. The doors swung behind them; some of the wind came in, and some of the leaves.

On such days Jack Leonard would come out onto his

veranda promptly every afternoon, at the first sound of a child's excited and breathless voice. Leonard had a stick in his hands; he leaned over the veranda railing and beat the stick hard against the resonant wood. The children yelled up at him "Old Jack, old Jack!" concealing their fright with derision. "Crazy old Jack!" they cried, and screamed and ran, while old Leonard's stick came down hard and curses came out of his mouth. In the house behind him, where he lived alone, the curtains hung in rags at the windows and a jumble of old crates and cans cluttered the doorsill.

The kitchen windows of our house overlooked old Leonard's garden and the long path leading up to Mrs. Parsons' door. Mrs. Parsons' path was the line separating our side yard from old Jack's slovenly rows of corn that were never cut down in the autumn, but were left to dry and later to freeze against frozen ground. Mrs. Parsons was a pillar of the Congregationalist church. Her son had gone to a military academy. Sometimes she took care of me when my mother went to the city. Her son's sword hung on the wall of the sitting room; a doll in a paper skirt, that held string, hung beside it. I used to look at these two objects for long unbroken periods; they possessed some significance that I could not pry out of them with my eyes or my mind. The doll and the sword were so pretty and so unexpected. The sword had a tasseled belt twisted around its handle. The doll's little feet under the paper skirt, the string appearing from the middle of a rosette in its sash, its bisque head and real hair and hard small mouth open in a smile—this was a problem I could not solve. As I remember my bewilderment, my judgment even now can do nothing to make things clear. The child has nothing to which it can compare the situation. And everything that then was strange is even stranger in retrospect. The sum has been added up wrong and written down wrong and this faulty conclusion has long ago been accepted and approved. There's nothing to be done about it now.

My mother's quick temper often estranged her from her neighbors. She was a woman of forty, beginning to be stout. She carried herself well and could be extremely handsome when she troubled about her appearance. She went about her life with an air of great secrecy and she was very much alone. She would stand, early in the morning, when the kitchen was floating in sunlight, beside the sink, cleaning the lamps. She had large, beautiful hands, but when she was tired or nervous she could not hold anything in them—everything she touched tumbled to the floor. She took up the scissors and cut the lamp wicks; she washed the lamp chimneys that were so prettily beaded around the top; she filled the base of the lamps with oil. After she had finished, she would stand by the window that looked toward old Leonard's house. The window had sash curtains over its lower half. My mother's gaze was directed through the upper, uncurtained panes. Sometimes she would stand there for a long time, perfectly still, one hand on the window jamb, one hand hanging by her side. When she stood like this, she was puzzling to me; I knew nothing whatever about her; she was a stranger; I couldn't understand what she was. "There's old Leonard again," she would say, "kicking the cornstalks."

The whole town, late in October, felt the cold coming on; in bleak afternoons the lights came out early in the frame houses; lights showed clearly across the river in the chill dusk in houses and in the mill. Everyone knew what he had to face. After the blaze of summer that had parched paint and shingle, winter was closing in to freeze wood and stone to the core. The whole house, in winter, turned as cold as a tomb. The upper rooms smelled of cold plaster and cold wood. The parlor was shut; the piano stood shut and freezing against the wall; the lace curtains fell in starched frigid folds down to the cold grain of the carpet. The little padded books on the table, the lace doilies under them, the painted china vases, and the big pictures hanging against the big pattern of the wallpaper all looked distant, desolate, and to no purpose when the door was opened into the room's icy air. The life of the house went on in the sitting room and in the kitchen, for in both these rooms there were stoves. If my mother happened to be on good terms with Mrs. Parsons or with Mrs. Gardner, who lived across the street, they would come to visit her in the early twilight, on those days when the lamps were lit at four o'clock. My mother made tea and the women sat talking in low secret voices beside the kitchen table. I sat in the sitting room, and heard their voices and the sound of dry leaves blowing along the walk at the side of the house. The two windows of this room also looked out over old Leonard's garden; at this hour a lamp was lit in his back room, behind a window covered by a cracked and torn shade.

Still with a sinking of the heart, I remember the look of that room shut away between the closed door of the parlor, where no one could sit, and the closed door of the kitchen, where my mother sat with a neighbor. "You stay here," my mother would say, and step toward the kitchen door, and close it softly behind her. Secrecy was bound up in her nature. She could not go from one room to another without the intense purpose that must cover itself with stealth. She closed the door as though she had said goodbye to me and to truth and to the lamp she had cleaned that morning and to the table soon to be laid for supper, as though she faced some romantic subterfuge, some pleasant deceit.

It was bitter weather, too cold for storms, too rigid and silent for the wind, when old Leonard first came to the kitchen door. Why he came I do not know. I heard his voice and my mother's voice answering, and I sat listening, not able to make out the words, and was terribly afraid. I did not dare to move from my chair; I remembered his strong old body, his fierce old face with a nose like a bird's beak, his ragged beard, the sound of his stick beating against wood, the curses coming out of his mouth. I could not call my mother or go near the kitchen door. After he had gone, my mother said that perhaps he had come in to get warm. "He's an old man," she said, but these words explained nothing to me. "He likes to sit where it is warm and talk to someone. You mustn't be afraid of him. He can't do anything to hurt you."

Every time he came, my terror hurt me to such a degree that I thought I could not bear it. I could not understand why he should want to come, or why my mother should want to open the door to him. I should have slammed the door in his face, put out all the lights when I heard his footsteps on the path, drawn down the blinds, pretending that the house was empty. I could not see how my mother could bear to sit in the same room with such ugliness, such age. One evening my mother opened the kitchen door, and I saw him sitting in the rocking chair beside the window. He was peeling an apple; he turned the knife round and round. His hat was on his head, and he said nothing. My mother had made him a cup of tea and put a plate of bread and butter beside it.

He lifted his head and saw me and grinned down into his beard. If he had put out his hand to touch me, I could not have been more frightened; with half a room between us, I stood transfixed by that smile. "It's Mr. Leonard," my mother said, and lifted the stove lid, shifting the kettle to one side. "It's a cold night, and I'm giving him a nice hot cup of tea to warm him up."

The peel fell to the floor and old Leonard closed his knife with his thumb. Then I heard him speak the first words that were not curses. "We must be wise," he said to my mother. "We must be as wise as the serpent and as gentle as the dove. As the serpent, as the dove," he said, and picked up the cup of tea from its saucer. The peeled apple lay on the table beside him.

These words now lie in my memory as inexplicable as the doll and the sword. I did not know what they meant then, and I do not know what they mean now. It is such memories, compounded of bewilderment and ignorance and fear, that we must always keep in our hearts. We can never forget them because we cannot understand them, and because they are of no use.

2 *Back through garlands*

Ꮶ Ꮶ The best time to write about one's childhood is in the early thirties, when the contrast between early forced passivity and later freedom is marked; and when one's energy is in full flood. Later, not only have the juices dried up, and the energy ceased to be abundant, but the retracing of the scene of earliest youth has become a task filled with boredom and dismay. The figures that surrounded one have now turned their full face toward us; we understand them perhaps still partially, but we know them only too well. They have ceased to be background to our own terribly important selves; they have irremediably taken on the look of figures in a tragicomedy; we now look on them ironically, for we know their end, although they themselves do not yet know it. And now—

in the middle fifties—we have traced and retraced their tragedy so often that, in spite of the understanding we have, it bores and offends us. There is a final antidote we must learn: to love and forgive them. This attitude comes hard and must be reached with anguish. For if one is to deal with the people in the past—of one's past—at all, one must feel neither anger nor bitterness. We are not here to expose each other, like journalists writing gossip, or children blaming others for their own bad behavior. And open confession, for certain temperaments (certainly for my own), is not good for the soul, in any direct way. To confess is to ask for pardon; and the whole confusing process brings out too much self-pity and too many small emotions in general. For people like myself to look back is a task. It is like re-entering a trap, or a labyrinth, from which one has only too lately, and too narrowly, escaped.

    K   K

I used to think that my life would be a journey from the particular squalor which characterized the world of my childhood to another squalor, less clear in my mind, but nevertheless fairly particularized in my imagination. When I see some old building—one of those terrible rooming houses with a milk bottle and a brown paper bag on nearly every windowsill—being demolished, I say to myself, in real surprise: "Why, I have outlasted it!" For it was these old brick hotels and brownstone lodging houses that I early chose, consciously as well as subconsciously, as the dwelling of my old age. I saw them, moreover, as they were in my childhood, with the light of a gas mantle making their dark green and brown interiors even more hideous; with the melancholy of their torn and dirty lace-curtained windows intact. Before the upper windows of some, an electric sign of an early vintage—of the kind that sported a sort of running serpent of red or green electric bulbs—was fastened; and I often have imagined the room behind or contingent to such a sign: the chair by the window, lit up by this fitful and pitiful light. Or I imagined my old age shut up in one of those brownstone houses, which, jelled in poverty, still stand on the upper side streets of cities. There among varnished furniture, grotesque wicker chairs, and dusty carpets, I would rock away my ancient days. There, if the downward sweep of fortune's wheel caught me off balance, I would end up; return. The old residents were waiting, shuffling up and downstairs in felt slippers; gossiping on the landing. The gas ring and the cheap frying pan, the improvised larder with its bits of food, the chipped enamel coffeepot and the saucepan for soup—all were there, behind some ragged curtain, waiting for me to return—to relive, in poverty-stricken old age, my poverty-stricken youth *in Ballardvale, a small town in Massachusetts, on the Boston & Maine Railroad.* . . .

A bare March sky with wind in it shed its light over the street; the gutters ran with melted snow under ice as thin as a watch crystal; last year's maple leaves lay matted on the lawn. My father and I walked down the hill toward the station, and said "Hello, how are you today" to Mr. Buck, to Mr. Kibbee, and to Stella Dailey. Old Jack Leonard had backed his horse up in front of Shattuck's store. A bag of potatoes, a ten-gallon kerosene can, and a black hound sat in the wagon, and a yellow cigar ribbon, tied to the whipstock, fluttered in the cold air. Across the tracks, the willows by the bridge let fall into the foaming water a mist of reddening boughs. The mill dam roared. The windows of the mill sparkled in the March sunlight falling without warmth.

The station platform was empty. Above our heads the station master's wife shook her duster out the window, under the scalloped eaves. On this platform, for nine hundred mornings, I have said goodbye to my father, and each morning he has given me a kiss smelling of cigar, and a penny, and I have looked carefully at the Indian on the penny's head, and at the wreath on its tail, and have remarked the penny's date. But now I am older, no longer at the age when one looks at the dates on pennies. I am going away. I shan't ever see again old Leonard, or Shattuck's store, or the hydrangea bushes in front of Forrest Scott's house that in autumn spilled dusty-blue petals over the grass, or the mill dam, or the mill, or the swing in Gardners' yard. . . .

We had come to Ballardvale from Milton, with no house ready for us to live in, and began by boarding at the Gardners'. My father must have been away, during those first few weeks, for I see only my mother and myself in the big guest bedroom, one window of which looked straight into the leaves of a tall tree. It must have been June or July, for I remember my mother sending me out to the little fruit store, down the hill, for a pound of cherries. And Ethel and I swung interminably in the rope swing in the yard. Ethel was a few years older than I was. I was seven that summer.

The Gardners' house was long and low; it had a higher central section, and two ells. It stood on a bank above the railroad tracks, separated from them by a sloping field, and a long strip of vegetable garden ran behind it. The front yard had several big maples, behind a white picket fence; and there were other big trees at the end of the house, toward the town. It faced the main village street, which rose rather steeply to a small white church at its top; and the houses opposite were of different sizes, painted white. (Later we were to live for several years in the big white house directly opposite.) The Gardners' house was painted yellow, and there were bushes on either side of the front door.

I can only express my delight and happiness with the Gardners' way of living by saying that they had one of everything. Up to that time (except for a short period before Milton) I had lived in the Milton Hotel; I had seen normal households only on short visits; I had no idea of ordered living. Households, in the New England of that time, as I later came to know, were often haphazardly equipped. The old was made to do, and the new was coming into existence little by little. The front parlors would have pretty ornaments, gilt frames, carpets, and cushions; the front bedrooms would have white bedspreads and pillow shams; but the kitchen was often still the center of the house, and often a disorderly "sitting room" lay between parlor and kitchen. Many people, as my mother would say, did not "know how."

But with the Gardners it was different. Order ran through the house. There were no bare spaces, or improvised nooks and corners; the kitchen shone with paint and oilcloth; the parlor, although minuscule, was a parlor through and through. The dining room, with its round table always ready for a meal (the turning castor-set in the center, the white damask cloth), was used to eat in, three times a day, and the meals were always on time. There was a delightful little sitting room, off the front porch. And beyond the sitting room, in one of the ells (our bedroom was above it), ran Mrs. Gardner's workroom (she sewed), with a long bare table, a dress form, and a cabinet-like bureau where she kept her materials. This was the first workroom I had ever seen. I used to dream about it for years.

Later, during the winter when my mother was away and I was in the convent, it was the parlor which enchanted me. It, too, looked down toward the railroad crossing, through the trees, and on its other side toward the front yard. A tiny curved sofa was backed against the window, with pillows at each end. The piano against the opposite wall faced the sofa; and a large seashell served as a doorstop. On the mantelpiece sparkled a row of hand-painted china. The white curtains at the windows were of net, with a lace border, and the rug had a small flowered pattern. Mr. Gardner's flute lay on top of the piano, in a worn black leather case; and there was a music cabinet with a small marquetry design on its doors. It was delightful to play five-finger exercises in these surroundings. But when we first came to the house I could not read anything—neither letters nor musical notes. The house was my book.

One of everything and everything ordered and complete: napkins in napkin rings; plants in jardinieres; blankets at the foot of the beds, and an afghan on the sofa. Pills in little bottles in the sideboard drawer (the Gardners believed in homeopathic medicine). Doilies on the tables; platters and sauce boats and berry dishes and differently shaped glasses and crescent-shaped bone dishes and cups and saucers and cake plates in the dining-room china cabinet. A brightly polished silver card-receiver on the table in the hall. A hat rack. An umbrella stand. And, in the kitchen, black iron pans and black tin bread pans; a kettle; a double boiler; a roaster; a big yellow mixing bowl; custard cups; pie tins; a cookie jar. Mrs. Gardner often made, for midday dinner or for supper, *one* single large pie. I can see it on the kitchen table, with juices oozing from the pattern cut in its upper brown crust. And I can taste the food: pot roast with raisins in the sauce; hot biscuits; oatmeal with cream; sliced oranges; broiled fish with slices of lemon and cut-up parsley on top, with browned butter around it. Roast pork; fried potatoes; baked tomatoes . . .

Ethel's father worked in the railway office of a nearby junction, on a salary which was fairly small, even for the period. But every move of the family was planned. Extreme economy must have prevailed, even with Mrs. Gardner's dressmaking money added to their income. No sign of economic pressure was ever allowed to show. Things were kept up, and cared for, but they must have been renewed, as well. Disorder was never allowed. The complications of laundry and of the personal toilet—for there couldn't have been a bathroom—were managed with precision and almost invisibly. The washbowls with the big pitchers sitting in them, the lidded soap dish; the towel rack with its long-fringed linen towels; the toothbrush glass and the tin of tooth powder—these, too, neatly existed. The long slender vase for flowers. The rough bristled doormat outside the door . . .

Blessed order! Blessed thrift . . .

ꗥ ꗥ

PRAISE OF MRS. GARDNER
BALLARDVALE, MASSACHUSETTS
(Circa 1904–1909)

Mrs. Gardner taught me to thread a needle and to put a knot at the end of my thread. She rubbed the thread end between her right thumb and forefinger, and the knot appeared.

Bless her for the threaded needles and the knotted threads. Bless her for her jellies and preserves, on the shelves *under the stairs* going down to the cellar. Jelly glasses and jars with wire fastening their caps. Green tomatoes with lemon slices (my mother did these, too). Red currant and the exquisite *quince* —with granular texture and indescribable color (pinker than apricot). Piccalilli—chopped fine. Apple jelly. Nothing mixed or uncolored. One by one she made them—or two by two— or six or seven at a time. —The chopping in the round wooden bowl with the crescent-shaped blade. The peeling. The dripping. The final wax and tin cover.

Bless her for the scrubbed pine table and the clock on the mantel-shelf—its peaked top and the little picture below its face. —Bless her for her coon-cat, whose tail, whose whole fur swelled up in the winter.

For her patchwork quilts, and for the doll hiding the ball of string. For her silver candy dishes, curly-edged and with handles, which always held some candy. For the three-layered gong in the hall—Japan, China?—so stylish for the time, that could summon to meals.

For her fringed linen towels on the towel racks. For her clean and dustless bedrooms, with the big water jug sitting in the big hand basin; the cake of good soap; the covered slop-jar.

And thank her most for the swing in the tree in the front yard: heavy twisted rope, wooden seat. The swing that could go high, and from which one had no fear of falling.

No fear, no fear . . .

No fear at Mrs. Gardner's!

↙ ↙

Perhaps one of the reasons why I hesitate to write of it is that, in writing it, I feel I shall lose it forever—and that I do not want to do. Not that moment, when I first stood in the door of Ethel's room, and saw what must, even at the age of seven, have struck me immediately and irrevocably: the order, the whiteness, the sunlight, the peace, the charm. It is at the door, looking in, that I always see myself, in memory: but I must have gone in more than once, and certainly the little objects which are the most precious part of my memory must have been observed close to, and taken up and handled many times. The dormer window looked out on the river, and had simple white curtains. The bed was under the slope of the roof. It, too, was white. I had never had a room of my own. This was Ethel's room.

Everything must have been white, even the furniture. It was a period when bedrooms had white painted bureaus, and the head and foot of beds (painted iron) were white, and little cane-seated chairs with prettily turned backs and legs stood about. . . . The bureau must have been low, perhaps with an oval mirror swung on two brackets above it; for I could see what lay on the top. Everything laid out with care, on the embroidered white linen cloth. A bolster pincushion, ruffled along its edge, stuck with pins, needles, and one or two brooches. The manicure things, laid in order to one side: scissors, file, orange sticks, and nail buffer—surely in the imitation ivory which was fashionable at the time. The china pin-tray, curbed and gilded at the edge, and painted with violets. The "hair-receiver," with a hole in its pretty cover, to match. The brush and comb, clean and set together. The buttonhook. The two tiny jars for paste and powder nail polish. The handkerchief box (I don't see this clearly, but I'm sure it was there). Then, last and most precious and beautiful, the ring tree.

Ethel had bracelets *and* a ring. I can't feel that she had more than one of each. The ring tree was made for several rings, but I can't remember any hanging on its minuscule branches. It was made of white china with a tiny green figure of delicate leaves on its saucer-base. The "tree" part was shaped like a leafless miniature tree, with at least three tiny branches —and a light scattering of gold, like powder, outlined its twig-like arms.

I go back to the house in dreams—or did, until the last few years. It has been changed—but it still has its beautiful self-sufficient air: a little low cottage, painted yellow—with its sitting-room windows facing the river. It still stands; I have seen it from the train.

I don't remember any books in it. But what a din I used to make on the piano! Learning to read notes is a part of Mrs. Gardner's. Learning to enter into the beauty of a spare but planned life, in which everything was used. No waste. No mess. No quarrels. No disorder. —I weep. I remember:

3 Back through flowers

🙢 🙢 I never remember either seeing many kinds of flowers or caring for them as a child. My Aunt Anne, I remember clearly, once showed me the little man in a bathtub, as she described it, in the center of a pansy; she had long been a children's nurse and this was one of her happy-making little tricks, I suppose. —Around the frame houses where we lived, in New England, or rather, bunched at one side of them and toward the back, grew masses of "golden-glows": rather like bushy yellow daisies; and we had bachelor buttons planted down the pathway of the house in Ballardvale. What was the matter with me, that daisies and buttercups made hardly any impression at all, although black-eyed Susans I thought pretty, and "blue-eyed grass" and the tiny flower of the low-growing cinquefoil (called "zinc-foil" by the Ballard-vale children) I remember noticing and bending down to look at closely. As a matter of fact, it was weeds that I felt closest to and happiest about; and there were more flowering weeds, in those days, than flowers in gardens—a sign, perhaps, of the whole rather depressed and run-down situation in the New England towns of the time, especially the semi-mill towns I grew up in. Yes: weeds: jill-over-the-ground and tansy and the exquisite chicory (in the *terrains vagues*). . . .

Terre vague—uncultivated land, filled with "chance vegetation." The unbuilt lots of my childhood, filled with tansy and chicory; sometimes with some scrub of trees. The three-family houses abutted on them; sometimes, even, yellow or red brick blocks with stores on the ground floor—such as we lived in in Norfolk Street. The wooden verandas in the back had these vacant lots as a view and a vista. Sometimes they were sunken, between two blocks of flats, and boys played ball in them in the evening. —The edge of things; the beaten dead end of nature, that fascinated me almost with a sexual fascination. . . .

I knew a few wild flowers: lady's slipper and the arbutus my mother showed me how to find, under the snow. Solomon's seal and Indian pipe. Ferns. Apple blossoms.

Pot plants in kitchen: coleus, begonias, geraniums—Easter lilies in pots, at Easter.

But the first time a flower really struck me as beautiful, strange, portentous, meaningful, and *mine* was in the room in a private hospital where my mother underwent an operation. Was it the year I was kept out of school, *after* the convent, or the year before I went to the convent? After, I think, since that operation marked a kind of limit to my mother's *youthful* middle age, and brought in the worse hopes and the lessened energy of a distinct later period. The Dr. X (that she had loved for years) must have been involved in this setup (the Yankee hospital, for example); and must have faded out from the picture soon thereafter, with consequent tragic reverberations.

In any case, the room was quite grand, as I remember it; not at all like a hospital: dark brown woodwork, a fireplace with colored tiles and a mantelpiece, a sunny window and wicker chairs. My father, my brother, and myself came on a Sunday. My mother was lying in bed in a pretty lace-trimmed nightgown, her hair in two braids. She looked young and happy and was in one of her truly loving moods, when affection rayed out from her like light. Someone had sent her a long box full of pink roses. Who could this have been? Not any of us.

I remember the roses, and disliking them: their long thorny stems, their innocuous color, and the asparagus fern in which they were packed. They seemed false, almost artificial, like wax or paper flowers; there was a touch of ill health about the curl and the veined color of their petals. The whole afternoon was rather frightening and forbidding; I sensed in the atmosphere that touch of "the other" world: of the conventional, Yankee world which I was on the verge of entering with real closeness, in which I would always have friends and allies, but also ill-wishers, if not enemies; the world of school and church then alien to me; of accents not quite mine; of genteel manners; of the *right* side of things. —The roses rather struck a chill into me—was I eleven?—and I found myself moving away from my mother's bed toward the fireplace, on the opposite wall.

Here is what I saw. Someone had put, rather casually, certainly, into a small glass vase, a bunch of what I now know is a rather common garden flower called French marigold. The flowers were dark yellow, with blotches and speckles of brown, and they had, I think, a few rather carrot-like leaves mixed with them. The sight of these flowers gave me such a shock that I lost sight of the room for a moment. The dark yellow stood out against the brown woodwork, while the dark brown markings seemed to enrich the sombre background. Suddenly I *recognized* something at once simple and full of the utmost richness of design and contrast that was mine. A whole world, in a moment, opened up: a world of design and simplicity; of a kind of rightness, a kind of taste and knowingness, that shot me forward, as it were, into an existence concerning which, up to that instant of recognition, I had had no knowledge or idea. *This* was the kind of flower, and the kind of arrangement and the sense of arrangement plus background, that, I at once realized, came out of impulses to which I could respond. I saw the hands arranging the flowers and leaves, the water poured into the vase, the vase lifted to the shelf on which it stood: they were my hands. A garden from which such flowers came I could not visualize: I had never seen such a garden. But the impulse of pleasure that existed *back* of the arrangement—with its clear, rather severe emotional coloring—I knew. And I knew the flowers— their striped and mottled elegance—forever and for all time, forward and back. They were mine, as though I had invented them. The sudden marigolds. That they were indeed sacred flowers I did not learn until many years later.

🙢 🙢

The life of the mind, growing up inside the outer life, like a widely branched vine . . . The individual *free* being, forced to begin small, like a sturdy shoot, but humble, which does not make much of a target for the wind . . .

When I wipe out all that I now know it is, there's little enough left. That little is incredibly solid, accurate, and to be depended on, built as it was upon the candid yet fierce intensity of a child's gaze, that knew all the tricks of sight; that could stop on the pane, to examine the flaws, the reflections, the colors in the glass, and could then plunge beyond, to gather up the texture of the opposite walls or the trees in the street; from which hints of weather, times of day, turns of the season could not be hidden.

People lived in intense worlds beyond me.

So that I do not at first see my mother. I see her clearly much later than I smell and feel her—long after I see those solid fractions of the houses and fields. She comes in frightfully clearly, all at once. But first I have learned the cracks in the sidewalk, the rain in the gutter, the mud and the sodden wayside leaves, the shape of every plant and weed and flower in the grass.

The incredibly ugly mill towns of my childhood, barely dissociated from the empty, haphazardly cultivated, half wild, half deserted countryside around them. Rough stony pastures, rugged woodlots, lit up and darkened by the clearly defined, pale, lonely light and shadow of weather that has in it the element of being newly descried—for a few hundred years only —by the eye of the white man. The light that falls incredibly down through a timeless universe to light up clapboard walls, old weathered shingles as well as newly painted, narrow-faced cottages, adorned with Victorian fretwork. In Ballardvale, the mill, warm, red brick, with small-paned windows (an example of good proportion, as I afterwards discovered); on side streets the almost entirely abandoned wooden tenements of the early mill town; on the main streets the big white or yellow houses with high, square parlors and bedrooms; the occasional mansard roof . . .

The people can only be put down as they were *found* by the child, misunderstood by, and puzzling to, the child; clumsy beings acting seemingly without purpose or reason. The grain in a plank sidewalk certainly came through more clearly to me at first than anything grownups, or even other children, did.

≤ ≤

I must have experienced violence from birth. But I remember it, at first, as only bound up with *flight*. I was bundled up and carried away. . . .

In the town of Milton violence first came through. I remember getting there with my mother by train; the name of the town was planted out in coleuses and begonias on a bank beside the station. I was four or five. We lived in a hotel, a long drive back through the streets of the town from the station. The hotel faced the river and the mill; a long rough pasture ran behind it. I played with the rough Yankee and French-Canadian children in this field. We ate rhubarb with salt, and an occasional raw potato. Downstairs in the hotel was some kind of barroom and café. The man's collar with a stain of blood on it, on the sidewalk, one Sunday morning. . . .

We ate in the dining room. My mother soon became friendly with the waitresses. She wore white starched shirtwaists with gold cufflinks, and sometimes drove over in a buggy to a dressmaker in a neighboring town; she handled horses well. A long, high blue mass rose above the trees. "Is it the sea?" I asked. "No," she said. "It is the mountains."

But it was fire which really attracted me. I had a toy stove, and matches. But I thought I would have some oil. So I asked one of the men for some oil. This brought on punishment and high words.

I also liked to hide and lose things. A little ring was pushed into the crack of the stairs. . . .

In spring the black walls of unpainted barns and of bare rock ledges, wet in the rain, had the same color.

The howl and whine of wind rose in the night. The high narrow houses on exposed hillsides, facing wide stretches of open country covered with trees, rocks, and bush, rocked in the wind. The weather changed unaccountably in the night.

The color of bare trees on the hills in March . . . The hillsides, once the snow had faded from them, had sunk into them, presented a color so bleached and so neutral that the color of massed twigs above them was warmed into purple—partly the color of distance, partly the color of bark.

How ugly some of the women were! And both men and women bore ugly scars—of skin ailments, of boils, of carbuncles—on their faces, their necks, behind their ears. Sometimes their boils suppurated. All this I marked down with a clinical eye. Then, their bodies were often scarecrow thin, or monstrously bloated. Mrs. X (one of my mother's "familiars") was a dried up, emaciated woman with a sharp nose and ferret eyes: a little horror. Later, I learned that she had carried on a clandestine love affair, for years, with the hotel's proprietor. I must put down his name: Bodwell. Like every other woman in these towns, at that time, she had a house full of veneered furniture, plush, and doilies; and she kept her sewing machine (again a custom) in the bay window of the dining room.

This was the town where I cut my thumb so badly, on a piece of bottle thrown out into the field. I ran to the brook and tried to wash off the blood. But it would not stop, so I put my hand against the front of my coat, and soon that was bloodstained all down the front. I was afraid to go home, but the blood frightened me more. I remember the doctor bandaging the thumb, beside a table, by lamplight.

And the town where the French and Yankee children—the girls—taught me their sexual games. Into these the boys were never allowed.

The secret family angers and secret disruptions passed over my head, it must have been for a year or so. But for two days, I went blind. I remember my sight coming back, by seeing the flat forked light of the gas flame, in its etched glass shade, suddenly appearing beside the bureau. What had I seen? I shall never know.

But one (and final) scene of violence comes through. It is in lamplight, with strong shadows, and an open trunk is the center of it. The curved lid of the trunk is thrown back, and my mother is bending over the trunk, and packing things into it. She is crying and she screams. My father, somewhere in the shadows, groans as though he has been hurt. It is a scene of the utmost terror. And then my mother sweeps me into her arms, and carries me out of the room. She is fleeing; she is running away. Then I remember no more, until a quite different scene comes before my eyes. It is morning—earliest morning. My mother and I and another woman are in a wooden summerhouse on a lawn. The summerhouse is painted

white and green, and it stands on a slight elevation, so that
the cool pale light of a summer dawn pours around it on all
sides. At some distance away the actual house stands, surrounded by ornamental shrubs which weep down upon the
grass, or seem to crouch against it. The summerhouse itself
casts a fanciful and distorted shadow. Then we are in the
actual house, and I am putting my hands on a row of cold,
smooth silk balls, which hang from the edge of a curtain.
Then someone carries me upstairs. The woman goes ahead
with a lamp. . . .

Then I see her again. Now the late sun of early evening
shoots long shadows like arrows, far beyond houses and trees:
a low, late light, slanted across the field and river, throwing
the shade of trees and thickets for a long distance before it,
so that objects far distant from one another are bound together. I never truly feared her. Her tenderness was the
other side of her terror. Perhaps, by this time, I had already
become what I was for half my life: the semblance of a girl,
in which some desires and illusions had been early assassi-
nated: shot dead.

4 Back through clearing

‮⊱ ‮⊱ My mother had true elegance of hand. She could cut an apple like no one else. Her large hands guided the knife; the peel fell in a long light curve down from the fruit. Then she cut a slice from the side. The apple lay on the saucer, beautifully fresh, white, dewed with faint juice. She gave it to me. She put the knife away.

(Or she would measure off, with one forefinger set across another, the width of some ribbon or lace which had run in rows around the skirt and sleeves of some dress she loved and remembered. "Narrow red velvet," she would say, or "white Val lace"; and the color and delicacy of the wide circles would be perfectly brought back into being. Or she would describe the buttons on some coat or winter dress: "cut steel" or "jet" or "big pearl." Suddenly all the elegance of her youth came back.)

Her hands were large and her fingers were padded under their tips. Their chief beauty lay in the way they moved. They moved clumsily from the wrist, but intelligently from the fingers. They were incapable of any cheap or vulgar gesture. The fingernails were clear and rather square at the tips. The palms of her hands were pink.

When she sewed, and that, in my childhood, was rarely, I could hear the rasp of the needle against the thimble (she had a silver one), and that meant peace. For the hands that peeled the apple and measured out the encircling ribbon and lace could also deal out disorder and destruction. They could tear things to bits; put all their soft strength into thrusts and blows; they would lift objects so that they became threats of missiles. But sometimes they made that lovely noise of thimble and needle. Or they lifted the scissors and cut threads with a little snip.

In Ballardvale a long path led up to the side door of the house, which led into the kitchen. At night, as you sat beside the table and the lamp, in the dining room, you could hear for a moment or two the footsteps of someone coming to that door, and, in the autumn, you could hear leaves scurrying down the path. You sat beside the lamp, which burned, without a shade, with a wide, flat flame.

My father's steps, coming home to supper, were reassuring. But there were others which were not. There were the steps of Dede, who sometimes came in the early winter evenings. I could hear her voice, and my mother's voice, in the kitchen, speaking low, so that I could not distinguish a word. Dede was dry and wizened (like Mrs. X in Milton). Her face had the ugly look of the queen of spades in a pack of cards. She wore a cotton wrapper, summer and winter, and a shawl was pulled over her head and shoulders: a mill woman's shawl, the use of which was dying out in the town. She lived in a dead-looking cottage up the hill, with her husband and a cringing hairy dog. She was confidante and, I suppose, go-between.

The kitchen clock struck. Why had Dede come? What was she saying?

Why do I remember this house as the happiest in my life? I was never really happy there. But now I realize that it was the house wherein I began to read, wholeheartedly and with pleasure. It was the first house where bookshelves (in a narrow space between the dining room and the parlor) appeared as a part of the building; they went up to the ceiling, and were piled with my brother's books, mixed with the books my mother had acquired in one way or another: from itinerant book salesmen, mostly, who in those days, in the country, went from door to door.

It is a house to which I return, in a recurrent dream. The dream is always the same. I go back to the house as I now am. I put into it my chairs, my pictures, but most of all my books. Sometimes the entire second floor has become a library, filled with books I have never seen in reality but which I have close knowledge of in the dream. I rearrange the house from top to bottom: new curtains at the windows, new pictures on the walls. But somehow the old rooms are still there—like shadows, seeping through. Indestructible. Fixed.

🖎 🖎

I began to read comparatively late, and I did not teach myself: I had to be taught my letters in school. I remember the summer I was seven staring at pages of print in bafflement and anger, trying to shake out some meaning from the rows of printed words, but it was no good: I could not read. But books were read to me, and I can remember the last occasion when this was done; it was during our first (and last) winter in the house on Oak Street, when I had scarlet fever, and was bedded down in the parlor for the length of the illness. My brother was home from school that winter and had not begun to work—he was nineteen or twenty. He and my mother were closer to one another, and gayer, than at any other time. They made a cookbook out of large sheets of brown paper, copying in the *receipts* by hand; and they laughed because so many directions ended by being placed under the heading *Miscellaneous*. My brother had been born when my mother was nineteen, and they had grown up together like brother and sister. He, too, had suffered his minor death, before I was born; he had been set apart from normal love long ago. Now he was a handsome young man, with great dark eyes; and that year, and for a few years thereafter, he was still capable of lightheartedness.

After my illness, I went back to school, and suddenly could read. I remember that early reader which was given to some of us, in the afternoon, as a sort of reward for a morning's good work. It was called *Heart of Oak*, and its contents were as delicious as food. They *were* food; they were the beginning of a new life. I had partially escaped. Nothing could really imprison me again. The door had opened, and I had begun to be free.

The first book I owned was *Grimm's Fairy Tales*—a thick

volume illustrated by Rackham, with a procession of figures printed on its cloth cover, which went around it, from the front cover, over the spine, to the back cover. This was enchanting; and every story became a kind of half-dream, half-fact. I believed that all this had happened: that the girl had let down her hair; that the princesses had gone each night to the castle on the island in the lake, and had worn out their shoes, dancing. The pictures (both colored plates and line drawings) *proved* the truth of the text. And yet it could not be true. I had the double vision of the born reader, from the beginning.

Later, when we moved to the house opposite the Gardners', I had worked out my escape with some care. The stove in the dining room stood out from the wall, and behind it, on the floor, with an old imitation astrakhan cape of my mother's beneath me (as a rug to discourage drafts), I began to read everything in the house. First came my brother's books—books whose names and whose substance I can never forget. *Cuore: An Italian School Boy's Journal; Cormorant Crag; The Young Carthaginian.* The coal in the stove burns steadily, behind the mica door; I remember the feel of the ingrain carpet against the palms of my hands, and the grain of the covers of the books, the softness of the woolen cape against my knees.

✒ ✒

My mother dealt with hot days as one deals with a problem of safety. When the New England summer came like a blast, over the town, so that the trees seemed to dry from their centers and held their leaves in the motionless air by an effort of will, she rose early, and closed the house. She never lay in bed in the mornings. Some sense of life (it could not have been a sense of duty) got her up and dressed and downstairs long before I was awake. "It is going to be a hot day," I could hear her say. She protected herself from the heat as from an intruder. The parlor shutters were closed; the inner blinds, behind the long loose curtains, which descended from the tops of the windows to the floor (where they lay in brushed-aside folds), were pulled down tightly to the sills. All over the house, the blinds were down. The wallpaper in the parlor scrolled its elaborate varicolored pattern (its reds and gold and greens) over the walls, in an artificial dusk. The cottage piano became a shape more than an object; the vases and the cabinet photographs on the mantelpiece almost disappeared in the gloom; the carpet (never taken up, even in the summer) lost its big islands of garlanded roses; the satin cushions on the wicker settee and the white doilies on the little tables alone showed up in the semi-darkness.

I remember a vignette of joy, one summer morning in the house in Ballardvale. I slept in the upstairs front room, in the big double bed, and I remember running from this room to the top of the stairs in the hall. I could see my mother, in a fresh cotton housedress, as she stood outside the front door, on the sloping lawn which ran across the front of the house. She was in one of her good moods. Was she singing, as she often sang, when these moods were upon her? What was it that gave that one moment, in that one morning, its distinction and delight? It must have been the first summer we lived in the house, for the next summer she went away, and I was sent to the convent in August. . . . The summer I was eight . . . Still open to joy.

In the hot afternoon she sat, by the parlor window, which

was now striped with light. She had put up the blind, and opened the shutters halfway, so that she could see and not be seen. She could look down over the sloping lawn to the sidewalk which ran beyond the maple tree and the fence. She could see as far as the Methodist minister's house (and little church) behind its tall unkempt hedge of *arbor vitae*; and, if she turned, down the street almost to the tracks and the river. She sat, shelling peas into a yellow bowl, or hulling strawberries. Sometimes I would sit in her lap, and smell the violet smell which was her own. . . .

When she dressed to go to town, the fear came back. She could not dress without scattering things about the room. Bureau drawers hung open; powder was spilled on the floor. She was careless (except in her rare spells of thorough cleaning) about the order of a room, but carefully elegant about her own person. A round cake of Roger & Gallet soap in the pretty soap dish in the kitchen; orris root in the drawers with her starched petticoats; a chamois skin for her rice powder; and a bottle of Peau d'Espagne. How I hated this perfume! It meant going to the city; it meant her other world; it meant trouble. . . .

She would bathe, in the kitchen. Then the crisp underwear went over her head; she pulled the strings of her corset and tied the ribbons in her corset cover. The long silk stockings, the patent-leather shoes, the shirtwaist of batiste or nun's veiling; the skirt, belled out around the bottom; the belt; the soft tie of lace at her throat. In those days, she still had her rings and earrings. One set was turquoise, surrounded by an edge of diamond chips. She put her earrings into her ears and the ring on her finger. She pinned a brooch at her throat. Her face, under its powder, was soft and mature; at the side of her cheeks, delicate down appeared when she turned her face to the light. Her lips moved over her teeth, when she spoke, in a way that warmed the heart.

She put on her hat and her veil, and lifted the veil down from the brim. She pulled the veil down over her face, and made a *moue* with her mouth, to adjust and loosen the veil (as though she kissed the air). How she loved herself! I have seen her come home from church and go straight to the mirror and there examine her face in the minutest detail, to see how she had looked in other people's eyes. Sometimes, when she was getting ready for church or for town, she would stand for long minutes, when she was already late, becoming more and more angry, the line of anger deepening between her eyes, while my brother or myself fastened her veil to her back hair, with a pin made of brilliants, shaped like an 8 lying on its side. She was always late. She blamed everyone but herself for her lateness. We had made her late. A dreadful chill came over our hearts.

A terrible, unhappy, lost, spoiled, bad-tempered child. A tender, contrite woman, with, somewhere in her blood, the rake's recklessness, the baffled artist's despair. . . .

Once, in Ballardvale, she was away for some weeks. No one knew where she had gone. Then suddenly she came back, thinner and, as I remember, in totally different (and shabby) clothes. She had a complete look of sorrow and of contrition in her eyes. Her eyes were humble; they asked you to forgive her. We forgave her instantly. She went about the house humbly and called us humbly by our names. She called (as she so rarely did) my father by his name. She swept and cleaned and changed the paper on the kitchen shelves. Then, after some days, she opened the piano and played and sang. And we (my brother and myself) sang with her. . . .

⩔ ⩔

My mother used to use the salt box as an index of time. "What will happen before it is used up?" What *did* happen—to her? I shall never know.

5 Back through distance

❦ ❦ *I am going away. I shan't ever see old Leonard . . . or the mill dam, or the mill, or the swing in Gardners' yard, or the maple tree in my own, or the hedge of arbor vitae around the Congregationalist church. Or hear, in the night, the express whistling for the crossing, or, in the daytime, the Boston train, and the train for Lawrence and Lowell, braking down for the stop, ringing its bell around the curve.*

Now, this morning, the Boston train is coming in from the fields beyond the river, and slows and brakes and stops. The steam shrieks out of the engine and smoke trails out, into the clear morning, from the smokestack, blotting out the willows and the mill dam. The conductor lifts me up to the step. That is the reason for my presence here. I took the Boston train in March 1909.

Boston was a city that possessed a highly civilized nucleus composed of buildings built around a square. These buildings were copies of palaces in Italy, churches in England, and residences in Munich. The square's centre was occupied by a triangular plot of grass, garnished at its three corners by large palms growing in tubs. The streetcars rattled by these. Perhaps, too, a bed of begonias and coleuses pleased the eye with some simple horticultural pattern. I can't remember clearly. It was the architecture which warmed my heart. The sight of imitation true Gothic, imitation true Italian Renaissance, and imitation false Gothic revival often gave me that sensation in the pit of the stomach which heralds both love and an intense aesthetic experience. And to this day I have never been able to extirpate from my taste a thorough affection for potted palms.

Harold Street, on the other hand, had not emerged from the brain of an architect of any period. It was a street not only in a suburb but on the edge of a suburb, and it was a carpenter's dull skill with pine planks and millwork in general that could be thanked for the houses' general design. Our house, built to accommodate three families, one to a floor, was perhaps two years old. Carpenters hammered new three-family houses together continually, on all sides of it. For several of my adolescent years, until the street was finally given up as completed, I watched and heard the construction of these houses. Even when finished, they had an extremely provisional look, as though a breath of wind could blow them away.

Sometimes I think that, between us, my mother and I must

have invented Miss Cooper; this is impossible, however, because of our splendid ignorance of the materials of which Miss Cooper was composed. We both lighted upon her simultaneously through the commendation of the drawing teacher in my school, who thought I was Talented, and Should Have Further Instruction. I was, it is true, thrown into a high state of nervous tension at the sight of a drawing board. This state passed for talent at the time. It must have been something else, since nothing ever came of it.

Miss Cooper lived in the Hotel Oxford, and I lived on Harold Street, and a whole world, a whole civilization, or, if you will, the lack of a whole world, of a whole civilization, lay between.

The Hotel Oxford stood a few yards up one street leading to the remarkable square. A fair-sized section of quarry had gone into its manufacture. And within it was heavily weighted down with good, solid woodwork, mahogany in color; with statues, large and small, of bronze and of marble, representing draped winged creatures which, although caught in attitudes of listening or looking or touching, gave the impression of deafness, blindness, and insensibility. (I thought these quite pretty at the time.) It was weighted with plush draperies, with gilt picture frames half a foot broad, with a heavy, well-fed, well-mustached staff of clerks. The little elevator, manned by a decrepit old boy in a toupee, sighed up through floors heavily carpeted in discreet magenta. Miss Cooper's studio was at the top of the building. It had no skylight and it looked out onto the railway yards, but it was directly under the roof; it had that distinction.

The big room looked as though, at some time in the past, the great conflagration of art had passed over it, charring the walls, the floor, and the ceiling, together with the objects they contained. Everything looked burned and tarnished: the brown pongee curtains; the dull bronze, brass, and copper; the black, twisted wrought iron; the cracked and carved wood of the Spanish chairs. Or perhaps it was the wave of art that had once washed briefly against it, leaving pale casts of the human hand and foot, life and death masks, a little replica of the Leaning Tower of Pisa, a tiny marble bowl surmounted by alabaster doves (the litter of art-form bric-a-brac) in its wake. In any case, there it was, and I had never seen anything like it before, and had it been Michelangelo's own workroom, it could not have been more remarkable to me.

Against this sombre background, Miss Cooper stood out like porcelain. She was smaller at sixty than myself at thirteen. Her white hair, combed into a series of delicate loops over her forehead, resembled the round feathers that sometimes seep out of pillows. Her white teeth, solid and young, made her smile a delightful surprise. She dressed in the loose Liberty silks which constituted a uniform for the artistic women of the period; around her neck hung several chains of Florentine silver. Personal distinction, in those days, to me meant undoubted nobility of soul. Distinguished physical traits went right through to the back, as it were, indelibly staining mind and spirit. And Miss Cooper, being stamped all over with the color and designs of art as well as by the traits of gentility, made double claims upon my respect and imagination.

It is difficult to put down coldly the terrific excitement engendered in my breast by those Saturday afternoons. I would come in, unpin my hat, lay off my coat, and there was the still life, freshly fitted into chalk marks, on the low table, and there was the leather stool on which I sat, and there was the charcoal paper pinned to its board, and the array of wonderful materials: sticks of charcoal, beautifully black, slender, and brittle; pastels, running through shade after delicate shade in a shallow wooden box; the fixative; the kneaded rubber. And there was Miss Cooper, the adept at these mysteries. Sometimes in the autumn evenings, after the lesson was finished, she lighted candles and made me tea. That is, she brought in from a kitchen as big as a closet, off the hall, a tray on which sat two cups and two saucers of Italian pottery, and a plate of what I called cookies and she called biscuits. Many times, after a cup of this tea, I staggered out into a world in which everything seemed suspended in the twilight, floating in mid-air, as in a mirage. I waited for the trolley car which would take me back to Harold Street in a daze, full of enough romantic nonsense to poison ten lives at their root.

Sometimes I wondered about Miss Cooper's own work in the field of graphic art. Pictures produced by her hand— pastels and water colors, all very accurate and bright—hung on the walls. But there was never anything on drawing board or easel. Every summer she disappeared into that fabulous region known as "abroad"; she did not bring back portfolios full of sketches, but only another assortment of small objects: carved wood from Oberammergau, Tanagra figurines, Florentine leather boxes, and strings of gold-flecked beads from Venice. These joined the artistic litter in the studio.

The enchantment worked for two years. In the autumn of the third, something had changed. In a pupil, the abstracted look in Miss Cooper's eye could have been put down to loss of interest; in a teacher, I could not account for it. Miss Cooper lived in my mind at a continual point of perfection; she was like a picture: she existed, but not in any degree did she live or change. She existed beyond simple human needs, beyond hunger and thirst, beyond loneliness, weariness, below the heights of joy and despair. She could not quarrel and she could not sigh. I had assigned to her the words and the smile by which I first knew her, and I refused to believe her capable of any others. But now, behind my shoulder, those October afternoons, I often heard her sigh, and she spent more time in the closet-like kitchen, rattling china and spoons, than she spent in the studio itself. I knew that she was having a cup of tea alone, while I worked in the fading light. She was still gentle, still kind. But she was not wholly there. I had lost her.

It is always ourselves that we blame for such losses, when we are young. For weeks I went about inventing reasons for Miss Cooper's defection; I clung to some and rejected others. When we are young, we are proud; we say nothing; we are silent and we watch. My ears became sharpened to every tired tone in her voice, to every clink of china and spoon, to every long period of her silence. One afternoon she came out of the kitchen and stood behind me. She had something in her hand that crackled like paper, and when she spoke she mumbled as though her mouth were full. I turned and looked at her; she was standing with a greasy paper bag in one hand and a half-eaten doughnut in the other. Her hair was still beautifully arranged; she still wore the silver and fire-opal ring on the little finger of her right hand. But in that moment she died for me. She died and the room died and the still life died a second death. She had betrayed me. She had betrayed the Hotel Oxford and the replica of the Leaning Tower of Pisa and the whole world of romantic notions built up around her. She had let me down; she had appeared as she was: a tired old woman who fed herself for comfort. With perfect ruthlessness I rejected her utterly. And for weeks, at night, in the bedroom of the frame house in Harold Street, I shed tears that rose from anger as much as disappointment, from disillusion and from dismay. I can't remember that for one moment I entertained pity for her. It was for myself that I kept that tender and cleansing emotion. Yes, it was for myself and for dignity and gentility soiled and broken that I shed those tears. At fifteen and for a long time thereafter, it is a monstrous thing, the heart.

6 Back through cities

🙋 🙋 (To the city): I came to you, a young girl, from a wooden house that shook in the autumn storms, and in the autumn I saw in *your* streets perhaps a handful of curled dry leaves.

I came at the age of the impossible heart, when the mind flew out to inhabit with warmth and compassion the rooms behind shut windows and drawn blinds; when even the advertising placards were invested with incredible possibilities of truth; when one watched the play of people's eyes and mouths, as though expecting enchanting glances, magical words, to come from them. . . .

❧ ❧

Perhaps the beginning of my "depression" can be located at the occasion (a fall-winter morning and early afternoon) when I went back to the earliest neighborhood we lived in after coming to Boston. It was always a good distance away, in one of the drearier suburbs, to be reached by trolley car from Dudley Street. But in those days (1909) the red brick block of an apartment house (with stores below) was surrounded by empty lots, and even, at the back, within view of a wooden veranda, by a scrubby overgrown field, filled with underbrush and a few trees. A large, sunken field was visible from the row of windows, on the apartment's long side; and here boys played baseball all spring and summer. The front windows (two in the parlor, and one in the adjoining "alcove") faced the openings of two or more streets, rather nicely kept, with single wooden houses—and even some white-washed stones outlining pathways. The brand-new apartment house, more than a block long, abutted on a small, older region, with some stores and a general run-down air. A steep street forked off to the right, downhill; and at the bottom of this hill stairs went up (v. close to house-walls) to the local railway station, with infrequent trains. I sometimes walked down this unfrequented stretch of tracks, on the way to school. The neighborhood finally reached by such a walk was already a semi-slum: depressing by reason of single houses needing paint, as much as by a scattering of those three-decker wooden apartment buildings, with front and back porches, which were becoming so usual in the outer Boston suburbs.

Our own apartment was of the "railroad" kind: a center hall ran from the front door to the kitchen, with parlor, parlor alcove, the large bedroom, the dining room opening out from it.

Beyond the kitchen (and its large pantry), to its right, and with the windows at the side (and at the back?), was a smaller bedroom, partially unfurnished, and dreary to a degree. My father and, often, my brother slept here. I slept with my mother, in the other bedroom, which had some respectable furniture in it, and a view over the open sunken field.

My father and mother, after a period of ghastly quarrels (and one long separation), at this time were making some effort to re-establish themselves, as a couple and as a family. New furniture and rugs had been bought for the front rooms; the piano was open and used; pictures were hung, and lace curtains veiled the windows. The woodwork of the place was, of course, dark brown, and dark green wallpaper predominated (although not in the bedroom, as I remember). There was a new brass bed. The dining room, where I came to do my lessons, had its square center table, its elaborate sideboard, a couch, and another largish table, which held some books and papers. The kitchen table was scrubbed pine. Was there a gas stove? The big black iron range functioned for major cooking —for those meals which often appeared at irregular intervals. I distinctly remember the taste of thin pieces of steak, kept warm in the overhead heating compartment, together with fried potatoes. Sunday dinner and the evening meals could be counted on to appear on time.

When I went back to this region, last fall, the whole area had slipped into true slumhood. The open field was gone; a large garage stood on its site: gray, metallic, forbidding. And the houses had crowded into the back scrubby field: a row of three-family structures, crowded as close to one another as possible. The air of a crowded necessitous place hit me like a breath of sickness—of hopelessness, of despair. The stores which had once existed in our block were gone: their windows cracked and broken. Only the old bakery, down the street, still persisted. The occasional sign was in Italian; a cheap pizza restaurant stood at the junction of the downhill street with the main thoroughfare, on which the buses now ran. I had walked down from Codman Square—the cross streets here had lost all vestige of the openness and quiet which I remembered; again crowded with run-down stores, with only the Public Library branch (where I had read my first books, in 1909) keeping a certain dignity. A large school building also abutted on the Square. This is now the Girls' Latin School, which, when I graduated from it, in 1915, was situated on the edge of the Boston Fenway.

A wave of despair seized me, after I had walked around the Library (now bedizened with cheap signs and notices but still keeping its interesting curved walls). No book of mine was listed in the catalogue. (A slight paranoid shudder passed over me.) —I felt the consuming, destroying, deforming passage of time; and the spectacle of my family's complete helplessness, in the face of their difficulties, swept over me. With no weapons against what was already becoming an overwhelming series of disasters—no insight, no self-knowledge, no inherited wisdom—I saw my father and mother (and my brother) as helpless victims of ignorance, wilfulness, and temperamental disabilities of a near-psychotic order—facing a period (after 1918) where even this small store of pathetic acquisitions would be swept away. The anguish which filled my spirit and mind may, perhaps, be said to have engendered (and reawakened) poisons long since dissipated, so that they gathered, like some noxious gas, at the v. center of my being. The modern horrors of the district also became part of this miasma; certainly the people in these newly overcrowded streets were as lost as those members of generations preceding them. Everywhere I looked, I saw *Death*; and I had to pass a strangely cluttered and disarrayed graveyard (new since my time) between the Square and my old house—(a home impermanent, it is true, for we lived there only two and a half years). But those were my first years of adolescence—and of the creative impulse—and of hard and definitive schooling. And, as I remember, in spite of the growing sense of crisis by which I was continually surrounded, they were years of a beginning variety of interests—of growth and of hope.

〴 〴

The thing to remember, and "dwell on," is the extraordinary *courage* manifested by those two disparate, unawakened (if not actually *lost*) souls: my mother and father. I cannot bring myself to describe the horrors of the pre-1914 lower-middle-class life, in which they found themselves. My father had his job, which kept him in touch with reality; it was his life, always. My mother had nothing but her temperament, her fantasies, her despairs, her secrets, her subterfuges. The money—every cent of it earned by my father, over all the years—came through in a thin stream, often blocked or actually exhausted. Those dollar bills—so definitive! Those quarters and ten-cent pieces—so valuable. (I went to school on a quarter a day.) Those terrible splurges on her clothes, which kept my mother going! How did they manage to keep a roof over their heads! With absolutely no plans for the future—no foresight— no practical acumen of any kind.

Yet out of this exiguous financial situation came my music lessons—my music—my Saturday money (50¢, often) for movies and even the theatre; what clothes I had—that we all had—and food. Even a woman to help with the wash. Little excursions to the beach in the summer.

No books (the library supplied those). No social expenditures. Those two people, literally cut off from any social contacts, with the exception of one or two neighbors—often as eccentric as my parents themselves. —No invitation to classmates—or perhaps one or two—in all those years. Cut off. Isolated. Strung up with a hundred anxieties. And yet they survived—and I went through my entire adolescence—in this purgatory—with an open hell in close relation. A hell which tended to blow into full being on all holidays—when my mother's multiple guilts towards her treatment of her foster mother tended to shake loose.

𝄐 𝄐

In the youth of a handsome woman, two currents and two demands run side by side in almost perfect accord: her own vanity's desire for praise and love, and the delight in the praise and love so easily given her. When these two currents lessen, a terrible loneliness and an hysterical dis-ease take their place. For the energy once expended on delight and conquest now has nothing on which it can be dissipated; it is continually meeting small defeats and rebuffs; it is like a river which has made a broad bed for itself, but now has dwindled into a tiny stream that makes hardly any show among the wide sweep of pebbles that show the boundaries of its former strength.

What was the first mood in their long anger, the first item articulated in their mutual disbelief, the first lie brewed out of their passionate dissimilarity? Sometimes, she thought that she might catch a phrase, as, after a long and lucid dream, we think that we can recount to ourselves the subconscious events with which we have so recently been involved. A sharp and stimulating tone—*taste*—remains: "It was *this*," we say to ourselves; but we cannot pin it down. At our insistence the flavor as well as the substance of the dream whisks out of reach . . .

If she could have remembered with clarity one word, she thought that she could forget it all—the sound, the look, the suffering—forever.

꿔 꿔

I cannot describe or particularize. Surely all this agony has long since been absorbed into my work. Even then, it was beginning to be absorbed. For I began writing—at length, in prose—in 1909; and within a year (my last in elementary school) I had acquired the interest of one of those intelligent old maids who so often showed talented children their earliest talents—opened up their earliest efforts by the application of attention and sympathy. I went to the Girls' Latin School in the autumn of 1910, at the age of thirteen, for five most fruitful years. I began to write verse from about fourteen on. The life-saving process then began. By the age of 18 I had a thick pile of manuscript, in a drawer in the dining room—and had learned every essential of my trade.

7 Back through silence

   Are you conscious, in your own writing, of the existence of a "usable past"?

Because what education I received came from New England schools, before 1916, my usable past has more of a classic basis than it would have today, even in the same background. The courses in English literature which I encountered during my secondary education and one year of college were not very nutritious. But my classical education was severe, and I read Latin prose and poetry and Xenophon and the *Iliad* during my adolescence. Arthur Symons' *The Symbolist Movement*, and the French poets read at its suggestion, were strong influences experienced before I was twenty. The English metaphysicals (disinterred after 1912 and a literary fashion during my twenties) provided another literary pattern, and Yeats influenced my writing from 1916, when I first read *Responsibilities*. The American writers to whom I return are Poe (the *Tales*), Thoreau, E. Dickinson and Henry James.

Did you find, in retrospect, that your writing reveals any allegiance to any group, class, organization, religion . . . ?

I was brought up in the Roman Catholic Church, and was exposed to real liturgy, instead of the dreary "services" and the dreadful hymnody of the Protestant churches. There was a Celtic gift for language, and talent in the form of a remarkable excess of energy, on the maternal side of my family. And I was handed out, as I have said, a thorough secondary classical education, from the age of twelve through the age of seventeen, in the public schools of Boston.

I did not know I was a member of a class until I was twenty-one; but I knew I was a member of a racial and religious minority, from an early age. One of the great shocks of my life came when I discovered that bigotry existed not only among the Catholics, but among the Protestants, whom I had thought would be tolerant and civilized (since their pretensions were always in that direction). It was borne in upon me, all during my adolescence, that I was a "Mick," no matter what my other faults or virtues might be. It took me a long time to take this fact easily, and to understand the situation which gave rise to the minor persecutions I endured at the hands of supposedly educated and humane people. I came from the white-collar class and it was difficult to erase the dangerous tendencies— the impulse to "rise" and respect "nice people"—of this class. These tendencies I have wrung out of my spiritual constitution with a great deal of success, I am proud to say.

Did you ever seek God?
No.

What is it that you sought?
I sought love.

And you sought love for what reason?
Those about me, from childhood on, had sought love. I heard and saw them. I saw them rise and fall on that wave. I closely overheard and sharply overlooked their joy and grief. I worked from memory and example.

Have you ever been alone, before this? Can you remember?
It is hard for me to remember anything by an act of will. It is my tendency to live critically, even hysterically, in the moment, without review or reference. But when I was not alone, I had a dream of nourishing loneliness. I saw it all, including the time of day falling through the windows. I sat in a chair, a book on my knees. There was no time of which I was the product or for which I waited. I looked upon this vision with joy. I can no longer.

Describe the configuration of the room, in the dream.
It was bare. Wide boards in the floor, a chair drawn up to the hearth, a tight bunch of flowers in a glass—

The insignia of luxury and leisure.
And of loneliness. The book opened upon the knees.

When were you ever alone?
When I was twenty-two and twenty-four, I lived alone in a

native and a foreign city. In the native city I occupied a cubicle and wrote for three evenings a week three pages, now lost.

PORTRAIT OF THE ARTIST
AS A YOUNG WOMAN

Sitting on the bed's edge, in the cold lodgings, she wrote it
    out on her knee
In terror and panic—but with the moment's courage,
    summoned up from God knows where.
Without recourse to saints or angels: a Bohemian, thinking
    herself free—
A young thin girl without sense, living (she thought) on
    passion and air.

The winds struck her; she flew abroad; what is this land
    wherein she wakes?
The armoire broods and the bed engulfs; the café is warm at
    ten;
The lindens give out their scent, the piano its scales; the trams
    rumble; the shadows in the formal garden take
The half-attentive gaze of the still-young woman, who will
    grieve again.

Everything falls to pieces once more; and the only refuge is the
    provincial stair;
People without palates try to utter, and the trap seems to close;
A child goes for the milk; the library books are there,
Generous to the silly young creature caught again in a month
    of the rose.

Is there a way through? Never think it! Everything creaks.
And here once more is the cold room, between thin walls of
   sadist and lout.
But at last, asking to serve, seeking to earn its keep, about and
   about,
At the hour between the dog and the wolf, is it her heart that
   speaks?
She sits on the bed with the pad on her knees, and writes it
   out.

In the foreign city I lived in a large room, surrounded by a
wide area of parquet floor and by walls bearing the images of
the Empress Elizabeth and two men climbing a snowy hill.
Beyond, the big Bechstein grinned in the deserted salon, full
of curled and dusty tinsel lace. Frau W. dusted the chairs in
the morning, peering at the woodwork and upholstery through
her lorgnette. She was a widow with a beautiful voice. She
loved an engineer in Baden bei Wien.

How did you occupy your energy and your leisure?
   Mostly in suffering. I suffered mindlessly, without reference to events, to reality, to time, then as now.

You did not note architecture, or the weather?
   Yes, I noted these always. I saw the afternoon shadows
deeply strike through the baroque windows, as I had seen
them fall, in my childhood, deeply slant and fall, drawing the
eye inward into unimagined interiors, through the wooden
joints and the wooden sashes that interrupted, in crass squares,
the lines of clapboards (under which, at that hour, the shadows deepened). I noted the excesses of plaster and the beau-

tiful horizontal reticences of wooden shutters. I saw the shadows lengthen to such a degree that the ground had no more place for them; they reached the walls, and spread upward, flat and definite, like unfruited espaliered trees.

You never sought God?
No.

What was it that you sought?
I sought love. Having been taught by memory and example.

By what means did you seek love?
I had no means. I was stupid, an exile in myself, sunk in a deep self-mirroring, self-effacing dream. I presented a still surface to the appearances around me, like a glass, stiffened into a polish capable of reflection by the same insane cohesion that keeps the particles of stone firmly within the stone.

You noticed? You observed?
The old man, in the spring mornings, swept together the fallen seed pods, sprayed out from trees, along the cobbles of the street leading down to the theatre and the bronze statue, itself defined against the light new leaves. In my street there was a pension, a brick hotel, and three cafés. It was a beautiful and a fallen city, smelling of mould, decorated with pediments on which bronze horses, their chariots, and their charioteers, leaped forward, in nineteenth-century arrogance; full of trees touchingly arranged along paths of beaten earth; full of cafés, courtyards, fountains, with broken statues wearing roses and crowns; the stone edge of their basins bore pots of geraniums; full of women's voices singing and the smell of fresh bread in the morning; full of the lumpy and the dead.

Through this you walked?
Through this I walked, wrapped in the deadening dream. Without memory or reference. But one night I remembered oil lamps, in the Redoutensale.

About you the ordinary world revolved?
I had early been stamped by the exigent demands of a childish loyalty. The beauty and arrogance close to me often met sneers and rebuffs from the less endowed beings about her. Early I saw them jib and sneer. Early, early, from the beginning, I abjured the ordinary world.

Deliverance rose in your mind?
Not at first. Not in the days when I stared with fury upon printed words I could not read, that I could not unbraid into meaning. I remember such a day. I took the book down from the top of the bureau: I feel the grain of the binding under my hand; I see the marks upon the paper; I feel my fury rising. —It was from these words that the deliverance later rose. But then they were closed to me.

How do you think that your apperceptions, your perceptions can be reproduced?
By chance, by indirection, by reference.

You are—?
The egotist who looks upon herself with joy. Like scales, cleanly, lightly played, myself rises up from myself.

Did you ever seek God?
No.

Describe the configuration of the dream.

It was bare. A small bunch of flowers in a glass.

And death and birth?

Sister Jerome died when I was ten. I gave birth to a daughter when I was twenty. My husband died when I was twenty-two.

Did you draw conclusions from this?

No.

What do you think of love and style?

They are both moving and ridiculous.

You were, perhaps, both a fool and a careerist?

Yes. In minor ways. I had the desire of surpassing the self through the self. But the pattern of self-abnegation was also strong. My sentiments, my sensitive, delicate, generous side made me a fool.

You had ambition?

I wished to live without apology.

You suffer?

No: that has been expensively excised.

You wished—?

To live without apology. . . . To live my life, at last delivered from ambition, from envy, from hatred, from frightened love, to live it until the end *without the need for philosophy*; that is all I ask. I fear the philosopher as I fear the ambitious, the seeker for God, the self-satisfied proud. In them lies evil. . . .

8 Back through lightning

❦ ❦

SCATTERED NOTES

The shadowy mother and the clear flowers
The flume
The mill: the smell of paper
Brother: blankets ready for school journey to Portland (cottage, hammock, fishing)
Turmoil: the lamp casts its light into a trunk with its curved lid up (the picture pasted inside).

The flume cascaded down the rocks, with bright sun sparkling on the clear, foamy water. My mother was afraid of the flume. It had voices for her: it called her and beckoned her. So I, too, began to fear it.

Years later I wrote of it. The poem came from the right place, and I worked hard on it, and it has some nice moments —the hot stove and the no-sound of water—which were actually observed and lived with at one period of my life. But I have never been quite sure about it. Perhaps I have the feeling that one doesn't get out of that kind of obsession so easily —the "facts" are false, at the end.

THE FLUME

I.

She had a madness in her for betrayal.
She looked for it in every room in the house.
Sometimes she thought she must rip up the floor to find
A box, a letter, a ring, to set her grief,
So long a rusty wheel, revolving in fury.
But all that she ever found was the noise of water
Bold in the house as over the dam's flashboard,
Water as loud as a pulse pressed into the ears,
Steady as blood in the veins,—often she thought
The shout her own life,—that she did not listen and hear it.

The fields had gone to young grass, the syringa hung
Stayed by the weight of flowers in the moving morning.
The shuttered house held coolness a core against
The hot steeped shrubs at its doors, and the blazing river.
She in the house, when he had gone to the mill,

Tried to brush from her heart the gentlest kiss
New on her mouth. She leaned her broom to the wall,
Ran to the stairs, breathless to start the game
Of finding agony hid in some corner,
Tamed, perhaps, by months of pity, but still
Alive enough to bite at her hands and throat,
To bruise with a blue, unalterable mark
The shoulder where she had felt his breath in sleep
Warm her with its slow measure.

                              In a mirror
Reflecting a barrow by a neighbor's barn
And a weather-vane stopped between north and west
She saw her face, as she had thought to see it,
Tightened between the eyes. She sat down on the bed
So that a tree was thrust into the mirror
Behind her head, and moved there shadowless
Turning around her the green of its distant leaves.
She had her two eyes before her, giving her back
The young face, softly marred by its own derision,
A hand that settled combs in the heavy hair,
The willing mouth, kissed never to its own beauty
Because it strained for terror through the kiss,
Never quite shaped over the lover's name
Because that name might go.

                         The tree moved over
Its bounded space, and gave some sky to the glass
Mixed with its leaves. Although the branch rushed loud
A field off, it was lost within the steady
Leap of the dam to the flume, made to a silence

She had heard it so long. Nothing against the cold
Beat of her own proud purpose was noise or power.

She had some guilt in her to be betrayed,
She had the terrible hope he could not love her.

II.

The wind before storm was to her the wind before thunder.
She heard the break within it from the first.
She never was afraid to face the heavy
Sprout of the lightning, for one moment branched
Within the sultriness of the high pasture
A little like another tree for a moment
Gathering through the window not like danger.
She ran about to shut the windows, slammed
The doors that gaped along the wall like ears
And tried to keep herself from the first crash
To follow the stripped spasm that took root
On the rocky hill, in the field, or in the water.
She needed more than a house to keep it out.
She clung to the wall, and smelled the dusty paper
Beside her face, and counted out the figures
Into a spell, to keep her terror hushed,
And clenched herself so tightly that she thought
Nothing could make her hear that noise again,
And again heard, spun down throughout the valley,
The spill from the long sky, over the roof,
Mounting as surely as the beats in pain.
The thunder was like agony, a smother
Against her life: she thought never to stand

Out in the free still air again, and buy
A loaf of bread out of the baker's cart,
Or cut the lamp-wicks in the early morning,
Or carry in the biggest lamp at night
Shining and clean under the china shade
To light the dishes of the supper table.

—Still—still—everything quieter then
Than the very earth escaping under the plough,
The depth beyond seed of the still and deep-layered ground
Stiller than rock, than the blackest base of rock,
Than the central grain crushed tight within the mountain.
It would be still again. She could say to-night
"There has been a storm," as though he hadn't heard
The hundred breaks within the murderous sky,
And he would say that thunder couldn't hurt her.
"There's been a storm," she would say. "Trees have been
    struck,
"Maybe a man stunned in an open field.
"The milk in the cows' udders curdled sour."
One woman frightened in a dusty corner
Who bit her fist and wished to pluck the thunder
From its swinging tree, to throw it down forever
Against the pastures it could not destroy,
And after the thunder, run and stop the dam,
The endless fountainous roar of falling water,
And scratch her heart free from the itching love
So much like sound, never spending itself,
Never still, in any quietest room.
The thunder ended. She could hear the others:
The water that wrapped the house like a shawly vine,

Love like a rough wind mixing a branch's stems.
The thunder had stopped. Some day she could stand
Listening yet, with the others silent around her.

III.

At night his calm closed body lay beside her
Beyond her will established in itself.
Barely a moment before he had said her name,
Giving it into sleep, had set the merciful
Bulwark of spare young body against the darkness.
Her hair sweeps over his shoulder, claiming him hers,
This fine and narrow strength, although her hands
Lie, shut untenderly by her own side.
Her woman's flesh, rocking all echoes deep,
Strains out again toward ravenous memory.
He lies in sleep, slender, a broken seal,
The strong wrists quick no more to the strong hand,
The intent eyes dulled, the obstinate mouth kissed out.
Outside the dam roars. He is perhaps a child,
With a child's breath. He lies flexed like a child,
The strong ribs and firm neck may count for nothing.
She will think him a child. He is weak and he will fail her.

Again she remembers the girl on the edge of town
Who took her lovers out along autumn roads,
Under half-empty trees, and shouted her laughter
To hear an echo thinner, later than summer's,
Answer her from the fields. Again she remembers
The true hard cold that caught at the wild girl's body,
When night after night she felt the autumn break
And open the country she knew, when she gave her kisses

Beside rough field-stones piled into a wall
Cold as the wind in every particle.
She had been that girl, this woman in a house,
Who well might have no bed. He had given her walls
She wished to burn, his body she wished to tear
Ever upon the knife of another's body.
He was the dark, he was the house and sound.

One morning she saw how the first autumn had changed
The splayed repeated figures on the ground
Making them leaves, and not the shadow of leaves.

IV.

She has been away. She shuts the heavy door
Against the stars of the late afternoon.
The fine fire in the kitchen warms the hall
And has turned the stove lids golden-red. Such burning!
Oh, equal to the terror of the cold
Biting itself outside, like a maddened thing,
Its tooth and fury matched. The lamp flames clearly
Against its glassed-in air. Nothing has changed.
Table and floor have been swept clean enough.
She pulls the frozen patch of veil from her mouth
And stands, like a stranger, muffled from the cold
To which she may return. Where is this treachery
That she has come home earlier to find
Wide in her house? It has not tracked the floors
Nor strewn crumbs on the shelves. It is hid away.

Begin to turn, you whirring stone in the breast;
Beat again, unsated pulse of fury.

He will soon be here. Give her before he comes
Whet to the blade. Lie open to her eye;
Rustle against her ear; give her mean glory
Of treason found outside the treacherous heart.
—No moon is close against the empty windows
To fill the cold hand of the air. The cold stairs murmur
In all their boards and nails, under her feet.
Her breath shows white over the lamp she carries
And sets by the bed. The panes shine back
As though there were nothing but a precipice
Beyond the wall, and the house itself a shelter
Held over space. She stands within the panes
As in the room, coated, the veil on her cheeks,
Save that there darkness streams behind her body
And through it. She almost knows the change
She could not know until now, so recently
The whistling cold outside beat down her sense.
But now she is snared. She tries to take a step
Toward the clumsily smoothed bed, and waits half-balanced,
Even her anger checked. Now all is over.
Her blood still beats, but everything else is still.
She stands in an empty room, in a silent room.
The ear has stopped. Great quietude spells the throb
Expected, because here the water sounded,
Because of it the bed and chairs stood here.
She stands here, too, because she once heard water
Night or day, go down in a bristling swing,—
Water now like stone over the dam,
And in the flume below, that once ran black
And marked its current with the earliest stalks
Of summer broken, the water might be the ground.

No longer the echo of frenzy bound on itself
Answers her from below. She and the mirror
Can play no longer together their bitter game.
Here now is silence, over the earth as beneath it,
The rim of the cymbal frozen, the drum gone slack.

And here at last the lust for betrayal breaks.
Her blood beats on, and her love with her blood
Beats back the staring coldness that would kill her,
Laying a palm over the ebb and return
Of her warm throat, heard now for the first time
Within this room. Soon he will find her,
Still dressed for flight, quiet upon his bed,
When he has hurried from the weighted cold
Toward the faint lamp upstairs. She will lie there
Hearing at last the timbre of love and silence.

↜ ↜

"To make oneself, and to be nothing but the self that one
has made—that is Existentialism's aim and end." Novels,
autobiographies, and critico-philosophical dissertations can
come into being through such aims, but never poetry. For
poetry must deal with that self which man has not made, but
has been presented with; with that mystery (by no means a
totally absurd one) by which he finds himself surrounded. It
is these gifts that the poet must spend his life confronting,
describing, and trying to interpret. It is not possible, for a
poet, writing in any language, to protect himself from the
tragic elements in human life. . . . Illness, old age, and death

—subjects as ancient as humanity—these are the subjects that the poet must speak of very nearly from the first moment that he begins to speak.

Poets, traditionally, historically, were those who asked basic (and unanswerable) questions. Who are we? Why do we live? Do we die forever?

WHEN AT LAST

When at last we can love what we will not touch;
Know what we need not be;
Hum over to ourselves the tune made by the massed
    instruments
As the shell hums the sea;

Then come the long days without the terrible hour,
And the long nights of rest.
Then the true fruit, from the exhausted flower
Sets, in the breast.

The practice of lyric poetry—the most intense, the most condensed, the most purified form of language—must be centered in a genuine gift. The chances of getting away with pure fakery within it are very small. One cannot fib—it shows. One cannot manipulate—it spoils. One cannot apply decoration from the outside; or pretend that non-feeling is feeling; or indulge in any of the lower-grade emotions, such as self-pity. The truth: and we can look back and see that piece of paper, in Dante, burning in the way paper always burns; and feel the coolness of Shakespeare's flowers; and the wet loops of Sabrina's hair. All immortal and all true.

But it's silly to suggest the writing of poetry is something ethereal, a sort of soul-crashing, devastating emotional experience that wrings you. I have no fancy ideas about poetry. It's not like embroidery or painting on silk. It doesn't come to you on the wings of a dove. It's something you have to work hard at.

THE ENGINE

The secure pulses of the heart
Drive and rock in dark precision,
Though life brings fever to the mouth
And the eyes vision.

Whatever joy the body takes,
Whatever sound the voice makes purer,
Will never cause their beat to faint
Or become surer.

These perfect chambers, and their springs,
So fitly sealed against remorse
That keep the lifting shaft of breath
To its cool course,

Cannot delay, and cannot dance—
Until, wrung out to the last drop,
The brain, knowing time and love, must die,
And they must stop.

When he sets out to resolve, as rationally as he may, the tight irrational knot of his emotions, the poet hesitates for a moment. Unless the compulsion be absolute, as is rarely the case, the excitement of the resolution sets in only after this pause filled with doubt and terror. He would choose anything, anything rather than the desperate task before him: a book, music, or talk and laughter. Almost immediately the interruption is found and the emotion diverted, or the poem is begun, and the desperation has its uses.

The poem is always the last resort. In it the poet makes a world in little, and finds peace, even though, under complete focused emotion, the evocation be far more bitter than reality, or far more lovely.

A LETTER

I came here, being stricken, stumbling out
At last from streets; the sun, decreasing, took me
For days, the time being the last of autumn,
The thickets not yet stark, but quivering
With tiny colors, like some brush strokes in
The manner of the pointillists; small yellows
Dart shaped, little reds in different pattern,
Clicks and notches of color on threaded bushes,
A cracked and fluent heaven, and a brown earth.
I had these, and my food and sleep—enough.

This is a countryside of roofless houses,—
Taverns to rain,—doorsteps of millstones, lintels
Leaning and delicate, foundations sprung to lilacs,
Orchards where boughs like roots strike into the sky.
Here I could well devise the journey to nothing,

At night getting down from the wagon by the black barns,
The zenith a point of darkness, breaking to bits,
Showering motionless stars over the houses.
Scenes relentless—the black and white grooves of a woodcut.

But why the journey to nothing or any desire?
Why the heart taken by even senseless adventure,
The goal a coffer of dust? Give my mouth to the air,
Let arrogant pain lick my flesh with a tongue
Rough as a cat's; remember the smell of cold mornings,
The dried beauty of women, the exquisite skin
Under the chins of young girls, young men's rough beards,—
The cringing promise of this one, that one's apology
For the knife struck down to the bone, gladioli in sick rooms,
Asters and dahlias, flowers like ruches, rosettes . . .

Forever enough to part grass over the stones
By some brook or well, the lovely seed-shedding stalks;
To hear in the single wind diverse branches
Repeating their sounds to the sky—that sky like scaled
     mackerel,
Fleeing the fields—to be defended from silence,
To feel my body as arid, as safe as a twig
Broken away from whatever growth could snare it
Up to a spring, or hold it softly in summer
Or beat it under in snow.
                         I must get well.
Walk on strong legs, leap the hurdles of sense,
Reason again, come back to my old patchwork logic,
Addition, subtraction, money, clothes, clocks,
Memories (freesias, smelling slightly of snow and of flesh
In a room with blue curtains) ambition, despair.

I must feel again who had given feeling over,
Challenge laughter, take tears, play the piano,
Form judgments, blame a crude world for disaster.

To escape is nothing. Not to escape is nothing.
The farmer's wife stands with a halo of darkness
Rounding her head. Water drips in the kitchen
Tapping the sink. To-day the maples have split
Limb from the trunk with the ice, a fresh wooden wound.
The vines are distorted with ice, ice burdens the breaking
Roofs I have told you of.

                              Shall I play the pavanne
For a dead child or the scene where that girl
Lets fall her hair, and the loud chords descend
As though her hair were metal, clashing along
Over the tower, and a dumb chord receives it?
This may be wisdom: abstinence, beauty is nothing,
That you regret me, that I feign defiance.
And now I have written you this, it is nothing.

🙠 🙠

The poet represses the outright narrative of his life. He
absorbs it, along with life itself. The repressed becomes the
poem. Actually, I have written down my experience in the
closest detail. But the rough and vulgar facts are not there.

9 *Back through smoke*

🖎 🖎   *Granted, then, that the traveller is here for an assigned, an established reason, the journey may proceed due west by slow degrees from the fireplace. Here I come upon two chairs that look worn to the bone, and a large, square green bureau, in execrable modern taste. The surface of this last is scattered over with objects of little real or artistic value. A sharp turn to the right brings me to the window, giving onto the brick wall before mentioned, and tastefully draped in dotted swiss. Then the entire west wall unrolls before the eye. The window is flanked to the immediate northwest by two pictures: one of a thunderstorm, and the other of a small bunch of violets. I then come upon a hanging shelf whose well-proportioned but inadequate interior can house nothing larger than a*

16mo. So that here all the 16mos in the apartment lie down together, the lion and the lamb: La Madone des Sleepings, Apologia Pro Vita Sua, *Whitehead's* Introduction to Mathematics; *the poems of Baudelaire, William Drummond of Hawthornden, Waller; the plays of Chekhov and Thomas Middleton;* Walden; or Life in the Woods; *The Turn of the Screw,* Montaigne's *Essays, and* Taras Bulba.

Beneath this truly horrifying array of literature is situated a large and comparatively unused desk, on which stand displayed pictures of myself and several other people, a pot of pencils, largely decayed, a cashbook that serves as a bill file, an inkstand that serves as a letter file, and a letter file that serves as a bill file. Also a lamp, an ashtray, a stamp box (empty), two postcards, a paper knife made out of a cartridge and bearing the arms of the city of Verdun, and a large quantity of blank paper. . . .

AUGUST 1933

My inability to write poetry comes to this: that I can write now only when in a rage (of anger or of hatred), or in a state which I can only describe as malicious pity. And the emotion that writes tender and delicate poetry is so much akin to the emotion of love that it *is* love, to all intents and purposes.

Yes, I remember very clearly the emotions, and their extraordinary resemblance to one another. The letting go, the swoon, the suffused eyes, the loose hand, the constriction in the throat, the abasement, the feeling of release.

Perfectly, perfectly, I remember them! But it would be a peculiar combination of overwhelming circumstances that could overcome my reluctance toward feeling either of them once more.

Abasement in religious poetry.

What one needs, when one has come to a state of this sort, is a bang up love affair that one can enjoy, and that one need not draw back from, or continually back and fill in. That's what one needs.

Otherwise, there's no hope, save a sourly smiling vigil waiting for the next rage to come on.

A dull life, really!

≪ ≪

SEPTEMBER 12, 1933

Five days ago I came back to America after 5½ months away. . . . R. met me at the pier. He looked pale, small, and washed out. He talked in an unbroken stream. He was immediately ready to defend his mistress: "There's no one I know that you cannot know. *Certainly* I'll bring her to the house."

All my determination not to let on and not to let go broke down when I saw the house rearranged, evidently with her help and in reference to her taste. All the logical, realistic approaches to the problem that I had built up in the early mornings, in Salzburg, with agony and tears, were swept away when I saw the well-bred and collegiate details of the rearrangement.

R.'s present situation is this, and there are reasons for it:

He is making a great show of love and appreciation of my return. Part of this is no doubt sincere. When I am *newly, freshly* present, I can for a short time represent to him a full and romantic emotion. This, of course, will soon disappear, and he will more frequently and more openly show

the resentment, the jealousy, the hatred that he really feels
for me in his heart. For a few weeks he will make a great
show of devotion and thereafter he will live more and more
apart from me, and again take up his dependence on the other.

And the reason for his continued romantic unfaithfulness is
this: he has no intellectual interests. He cannot read, he
cannot judge, he cannot analyze or plan. So he waits for the
newest wind of romantic love to blow over him, and again
and again writes a new series of sonnets, in which the stars
bend from heaven and sink into his beloved's eye. His life
is again rescued, blessed and refreshed by a new woman.
Nothing, in his actions, seems to him strange, or disloyal, because he cannot detach himself from the adolescent image
he has of himself: the passionate lover, the poet drowned in
his lover's arms.

To live with this kind of moral and emotional insanity
is hideous. I cannot understand the reasons why I cannot
at once break away. But I must admit to myself that I need
devotion, even the devotion of a confused and mindless bundle
of unresolved emotions like Raymond. I am not yet ready to
stand by myself, so I share his bed, revile his character and
endeavor to build my work on this unsteady basis. The
situation could not fit the needs of my own obsessions better
if it had been planned for them (to complete them) by some
fiendish omniscient being. The distrust, the insecurity I feel
shatters me open like repeated blows, and yet, at the present,
I can do nothing, I am unable to *will* anything, in order to get
away.

O God, give me this power this year!

Well, there is the situation as it now stands. It is my life
as it now stands: I must examine it, but not let it hinder me

or destroy me. Today—on September 12, 1933—I have the perhaps mistaken illusion that somehow the necessary change will come about by my own deed. But I may die with a gallery of R.'s romances all about me, with his latest sonnets to his latest star-lit love singing in my ears. It may be like that. Perhaps my fundamental weaknesses, or the profound fatigue of will that struck me eight or nine years ago (the result of turmoil—unspeakable turmoil—suffered in childhood, youth and early maturity) will make me strong through it all and suffer it all and endure it all.

I am tired. I have much work to do. I don't know.

I put all this down in order to clarify my own heart. I have never been able to set down the intricacies of such a personal situation before. Here let it stand, as a part of my life. I, the woman who has finally abandoned her own romantic hopes, her own corroding dreams, who wishes for nothing but the continuance of a will to work, some food, shelter, clothing, and a good library—who at last has no longer any need of sympathetic friends, in confidants, who stands in this world as though she were already dead to its actions and its tumult, if not to its torment.

If *you* could only love again! Not be loved, but *love*. At least R. is free of *that* disease, and perhaps, after all, healthier than you. Perhaps you are the canker, the lichen, the dry rot of life, and he is the sunny victor.

ᔕ ᔕ

SEPTEMBER 15, 1933

. . . Ten thousand resolutions to the contrary do me no good:

I am still at the mercy of my neurotic pride, a pride that, in certain manifestations, closely approximates insanity. For the first time in my life I admit the pathological implications in that pride. And at the same time I admit that I need some hand over me, for the present at least, although the hand be weak. I know R. to be a victim of Shelleyism and a person who can ultimately do me no good. But I also admit that I feel for him a kind of personal need: I have lived with him for so long that he has become almost like a fifth limb, like a member of my body. And I need even the imperfect love that he can give me. Along with the rest of the poor deracinated generation who in childhood saw the end of one sort of life and who in early maturity, by the turmoil of their lives, helped to form this new, childish, incomplete existence in which we are forced to live, I need some love, however imperfect.

My own insistence upon honor and maturity and decency may be merely a defence against the world. I cannot, all at once, become a detached self-delighting individual. My own ideas are steeped in a romantic brew, however much I hate the color and the stain. I was fed on nineteenth-century literature, on symbolist poetry, on provincial morality. My two defences against the nonsense in myself and in others are my realism and my wit. Perhaps I can keep some inner balance with the help of these two, and with the help of routine and *willed* creation.

God keep me sane, and God help me to produce and to grow.

✎ ✎

Sparrow said to me: You are resting on your laurels. You are finished. You are mummified. Take off your earrings and do some work. You didn't go about being a visible specimen of a fine high-stern woman, well dressed and keeping her chin up, when you produced your early poetry. Look at the people about you, whom you often fear. They will be dead and forgotten and unmarked. But you and I are immortal. The only immortality is in the printed word. Get going.

ɞ ɞ

COMING OUT

Going in is like this: one morning you finally make up your mind that no one in the world, with the single and certain exception of yourself, has a problem, utters a groan, or sheds a tear. The entire habitable globe, to your distraught imagination, is peopled by human beings who eat three meals a day, surrounded by smiling faces, work with a will in offices, fields, factories, and mines, and sleep every hour of the night. All the young human beings are in love; all the middle-aged are either charmingly drunk or soberly busy; all the old are reading memoirs or knitting or whittling wood, completely jolly and resigned. The animal world, as well, gambols about in jungle and over llano and crag; happy bright-eyed sheep crop grass; the gay cow chews its cud; the laughing crow swoops over the cornfield. Fish and mussel, ant and peacock, woodchuck and mole, rabbit and cuttlefish go their several ways rejoicing. The cat on the hearth conceals no tattered heart beneath its fur, and the dog on the leash is ravaged by neither remorse nor despair.

You look back over history and it presents to your biased eye nothing but records of glamour and triumph. O happy

happy Aztecs; O splendid Punic Wars; O remarkably situated medieval serfs; O Renaissance figures, armed to the teeth and glowing with inward delight; O fortunate members of the Children's Crusade; O jolly dwellers in the fifteenth, sixteenth, seventeenth, and eighteenth centuries! O Athenians, O Mongols, O Seljuk Turks, Semites, Visigoths, Manchus, Moors, and paleolithic woman and man! Happy, happy they!

As for you, the most miserable person in any age, you sob and clutch your breast and reject with a sneer all consolations of religion and philosophy. You kick, you snarl, you spit, and you scream. Outside your horrid home the peaceful world flows serenely by: traffic lights change, and the streetcars, instead of swerving off the tracks under the influence of a motorman in the throes of anguish, stop quietly at a lifted hand. People go from one place to another and seem equally pleased with either. Men and women, living their lives neatly and with hellish certainty and precision, rise in the morning, bathe, dress, eat breakfast, lunch, and dinner, smoke cigarettes, earn their livings, drink cocktails, brush their teeth; and, after a well-spent day, finally retire. Looms chatter, turbines whir, and automobiles consume gasoline (for, to your disordered mind, even the machines are happy). In the bowels of the earth miner does not attack miner with shovel and pick; sanely, and in an orderly fashion, all miners attack the coal, iron, or other mineral which they are expected to attack. The captains of ships do not furiously hurl their instruments of navigation clear across the bridge. No barricades are thrown up in the streets, and, in motion-picture and other theatres, the imperturbable patrons would never think of breaking into a howl and charging, in a body, the stage or screen.

Elsewhere, all is mild. But for you there is no hope. Your

nervous system yawns before you like the entrance to the pit and you are going in.

The period of time over which you harbor these mistaken ideas about yourself and the rest of the world varies greatly. If your constitution is good, you may easily growl and snarl for the rest of your life. If you are of feeble stamina, you may sob and scratch for perhaps two months or two years. In order to give this article some point, let us assume that, after a reasonable lapse, you finally recover. A remnant of your life lies before you. You can choose several roads to happiness and a useful career. Let us examine these roads as briefly as possible.

You may, with great rapidity, start hating or loving. Your love may be of the Shelleyan or of the Christian variety: you may, on the one hand, sink infatuate on the breast of one individual (or, progressively, upon the breasts of several, in a series); on the other, you may figuratively embrace all mankind. Hate does not present many choices; if hate is your solution, you are fairly certain to hate all phenomena with equal joy and intensity, without troubling to drag into prominence any one feature from the loathsome whole. Or you may feel very noble or very powerful. Feeling noble or powerful also defies analysis; when one feels noble or powerful in any degree, one feels noble or powerful, and there's nothing more to say.

But no matter how rapidly you manage to go into your adjustment, no matter how eagerly you grab at the sops of love, hate, nobility, or the passion for personal dominance, you are certain to see, for one lucid moment, one clear flash of that world formerly thought so serene. For one split second you are upheld in a dead calm. You are no longer the world's lost child or the universe's changeling. You are a normal person, ready to join your fellows.

Standing on the latest point reached in the long and unbroken graph of lunacy that rises from the eoliths and culminates, for the time being, in the general situation at whatever day, hour, minute it happens to be, you may survey those fellows from whom you have long felt yourself estranged. You will survey them, I trust, with affection, or with malicious pity; it is not the part of a noble and newly normal soul to survey them with contempt. You will survey the intelligent unhinged, the unenlightened witless, and the plain cracked. And you will realize (only for a moment, you understand) that if you took to eating blotting paper, painting things green, living in trees, or indulging in frequent, piercing maniacal cries, you could not exceed the high average of oddity and derangement that you perceive all about you.

Having had your moment, you no longer have anything to fear. Crawl in and out of your nervous system as you will, you are an initiate. You are among friends. You are cured. You may again take your place as a normal person in a normal world.

✍ ✍

OCTOBER 19, 1933

The horror of Virginia's life and Virginia's room. Old age finally crowded into a narrow box: sixty-five cents spending money. The lending library. The cafeterias so near that one can walk to them on a cold winter night with ease. What does she do with herself all day? She lies on the narrow bed and reads: reading has become a drug and a mania with her. She comes into a room and scours the tables and shelves for something to read.

But I *could* not live through such horror. I could not. The thought of my own possible suicide, under certain conditions, is becoming more and more clear in my mind. Old, poor, alone, it is not possible. The series of boxlike little rooms on the 11th floor.

What have I to make me unhappy, after that? What effect can "What people say," a husband's bungling infidelity, a lessened joy in life, an imperfect ambition, have on a woman who is still young and has enough money to buy cigarettes and new dresses? But Virginia must be *somehow* happy— what is it?—or she couldn't stay alive.

✒ ✒

At the newsreel theatre—
I said to myself: Very well, why should I not let down and become part of this? How ridiculous I am here, in my isolation and my half-elegance—the hair straight and pushed back from the face, the black dress, the purse, the gloves. Here are statesmen, strike leaders, tennis players—their loose mouths, their jagged teeth, their eyes too close together, their words enunciated like peasants. Here stands Mussolini, already grizzled, an aging bullet-headed man. Convicts have wrecked a prison. The fleet shoots off guns. The rayon, silk, and woollen textile workers are ordered to stand by for further instructions. Children laugh at monkeys. Here are residents of Papua, clasped in a beautiful and friendly dance, with impassive faces and linked arms; the officers of the cruise

ship give them jars of jelly which they receive with great deference.

Let down—believe—be part of it. O disordered, meaningless life! Let down! But I could not.

ᘏ ᘏ

EVENING IN THE SANITARIUM

The free evening fades, outside the windows fastened with
    decorative iron grilles.
The lamps are lighted; the shades drawn; the nurses are
    watching a little.
It is the hour of the complicated knitting on the safe bone
    needles; of the games of anagrams and bridge;
The deadly game of chess; the book held up like a mask.

The period of the wildest weeping, the fiercest delusion, is
    over.
The women rest their tired half-healed hearts; they are almost
    well.
Some of them will stay almost well always: the blunt-faced
    woman whose thinking dissolved
Under academic discipline; the manic-depressive girl
Now leveling off; one paranoiac afflicted with jealousy.
Another with persecution. Some alleviation has been possible.

O fortunate bride, who never again will become elated after
    childbirth!
O lucky older wife, who has been cured of feeling unwanted!

To the suburban railway station you will return, return,
To meet forever Jim home on the 5:35.
You will be again as normal and selfish and heartless as
    anybody else.

There is life left: the piano says it with its octave smile.
The soft carpets pad the thump and splinter of the suicide to
    be.
Everything will be splendid: the grandmother will not drink
    habitually.
The fruit salad will bloom on the plate like a bouquet
And the garden produce the blue-ribbon aquilegia.

The cats will be glad; the fathers feel justified; the mothers
    relieved.
The sons and husbands will no longer need to pay the bills.
Childhoods will be put away, the obscene nightmare abated.

At the ends of the corridors the baths are running.
Mrs. C. again feels the shadow of the obsessive idea.
Miss R. looks at the mantel-piece, which must mean
    something.

℘ ℘

    All that winter in the afternoon at four o'clock precisely
the voice ran through the halls. "Walking, walking," it cried,
with a sort of falsely cheerful note of invitation, an affected
note of persuasion. Everyone promptly appeared, a few moments after the call, their hats and gloves already on, and

more or less warmly clad, according to the state of the weather. The young women from the Physical Education Department were invariably young, brisk, and slender; they wore short skirts, leather jackets, bright mittens, and bright woolen socks. They walked into the rooms of the laggards. The laggards got into their hats and coats and came along.

When everyone was ready, the nurse unlocked the door, and the group went out into the hall and down the stairs. This outer hall was completely bare; the plaster looked desolate and bleak in the light falling through the grilled windows. The stairs were of iron and concrete. But it was good to see the outer hall; it was pleasant to be going out into the air. Some of the women were worried or elated about the kind of day it was. But most of them had come to a point where the weather did not matter.

Even in winter the grounds in front of the main building had the look of a well-kept park. Many trees grew up from the wide lawn and the stretch of dry winter grass was broken by bushes and the outlines of flower-beds. The three convalescent groups from the halls, who alone were candidates for the walk, met near the bare and thread-like branches of an ornamental tree that bent over toward the ground in a kind of veil, sensitive to the winds of January, February, and March. Sometimes there was snow beneath these branches, and always, when there was sun at all, the unfinished-seeming rays of late afternoon light lay upon the walls of the long red brick building, and upon the gravel paths, and made shadows with the trees upon the ground.

The groups always had their happy members, who ran toward each other with friendly cries. Very nearly everyone chose a partner; few stood silent with their heads turned away. One young woman in a leather jacket led the way, at the head of the line; another embedded herself halfway along, and one brought up the rear. Now some women and girls linked arms; the happiest lot rushed toward the front; the quieter ones followed them.

They walked down the sweep of driveway. They passed the house of the director of the hospital, and there were always some who laughed at his wife's choice of window curtains, and some who made as if to peer into the dining room windows, where decanters and cruets were visible on the sideboard. They passed the houses of the other doctors, and some of these were new, built of bright brick and white-painted wood, in a Tudor cottage design. Behind these little brick cottages the land fell away, and a view of a steep uphill road could be seen, between the trees. The distant road went uphill between rows of telegraph poles, and at the top of the hill, against the winter sky, stood some frame houses and a large building that looked like a powerhouse. This was a street on the outskirts of the town, that seems to begin and end nowhere.

Soon the concrete sidewalk came to an end, and a broken, uneven walk of asphalt began. The asphalt had broken into queer holes and pools, and most of the women, at one time or another, had learned their shapes by heart. At the end of the asphalt walk, the dirt road began, and from that point onward, the scene took on the look of a neglected countryside. To one side there was a small, ragged wood, without undergrowth, and on the other, at the bottom of the hill, lay a small pond. Beyond the pond was a wall, and beyond the wall the town began again. Here, also, it rose above eye level, and the steep streets presented a row of apartments, of an artistic, half-muted design to the sight. Far away, in the distance, the higher buildings of the town rose. A hotel was the highest building of all, and anyone could read the letters of the big electric sign on its roof, if they took the pains, even though the sign read backward, since it was the back of it which could be seen from the hospital grounds.

Everyone became brighter or gloomier as soon as the apartment houses came into view. They saw them at the hour of the day's turning point, when all has been done that can be done, when effort gives way to plan and to dream, when the lamp stands ready to be switched on. The hour when children begin to scent supper. The hour when the husband's foot is nearly outside the door. The walking women knew the hour in their bones. It was no hour for women to be out, taking an aimless walk.

At this moment of the walk Miss Andrews heard again inside her heart her father's voice; he admonished her; he looked at her with love. Little Mrs. Harburg felt the fear that nothing could happen again; that everything was over; that life had closed up against her. Mrs. Shields saw again the face of her husband, that denied her, and felt his shoulder, turning strongly, unhurriedly away from her arms. The young girls felt a flood of wildness and fear go over them; the older women saw the monotonous afternoon light recede away from them, like a tide going out that reveals the ugliness of the beach. At this point Miss Gill heard the voice that told her she must run away. Her plan, to get rid, forever, of her sagging and unused body. Some heard or saw nothing, but felt again that pang, nameless and centered below the throat, of sorrow which had become part of them, like an organ in their flesh. Some began to listen to the old story of suspicion and thwarted love, always told in the same words, always ending in a question and an answer they could not bring themselves to acknowledge. Over and over, in the groove worn into their minds, the terrible certainty loosened and moved. That which could not happen, but had happened; that which could not be borne, but which they were bearing.

Sometimes the pond was frozen over, and stared at the air with an icy reflection, and sometimes it was water, perfectly calm or moving under the wind. The women walked down-hill, now in a more ragged line. They turned toward the little clump of trees, and now they seemed somewhat gayer, al-though many had fallen behind, singly, or by twos and threes. Last autumn's leaves lay thickly on the path, together with tufts of faded weeds. The girls at the head of the line had already reached the wooden bridge over the dried stream, and stood leaning against its railing, laughing together. A young woman in bright mittens went back to hearten the stragglers, and presently the whole group stood upon the bridge. They stood in two rows, on opposite sides, and looked at each other.

This pause in the walk brought some comfort to them all. They had turned away from the houses of the town. They see and recognize things about each other. The inner sounds snapped silent, and they again heard each other, and the gossip and jeering of their gayer companions. The outer cer-tainty—the bridge, the path that from here pointed back to the hospital, the faces of the others, their clothes and their manner of speech—covered up the terrible inner sounds and appearances. This, too, was a world; they were able to use and to recognize it. But Miss Gill never for a moment, out of the corner of her eye, lost sight of the gate in the distance, through which, if she were clever, one day she would run, and Miss James felt the guilt rise against her, and heard someone cry, very loud, "You fool, you fool!"

Then they turned into the long field, along the rough

cinder road. Here it was cold, and the wind took them, and hurried them along. They hurried under the branches of the broken orchard, beside the ploughed field which in summer was a kitchen garden; they reached the top of the hill once more and saw the doctors' and nurses' cars lined up behind the old stables. It was getting darker. The whole cold sky, whether lowering with one cloud, or else clear with the white light of winter, darkened at the zenith and toward the east. They swung back onto the concrete walk, and up the drive-way. The long hospital building stood before them, and soon they would have tea.

They had gone such a short distance, but no matter how often they took that journey, they were puzzled again that this should be the end of it; that wherever they had been, they should be made to come back here.

✍ ✍

Now I am somewhat better, and this week I go back to town for the first time, in order to discover what life is perhaps/ really like outside clinic walls. Perhaps, in the main, the process of partial disintegration is salutary, and even necessary, when sensitive people reach their middle thirties. A good look into that abyss described by so many—Pascal, Dante, Sophocles, Dostoevsky, to name a few—but never really grasped by the mind until experienced by the emotions with some expenditure of blood and tears—such a glance is all to the good, I am sure. It's just as well to know that the ninth circle has an icy floor by experience: by having laid the living hand upon it.

10 *Back through hours*

🖎 🖎   The keeping of a journal may become a futile and time-wasting occupation for a writer. Temptations toward the inconsequential detail, the vaporous idea, and the self-regarding emotion are always present and can become overwhelming. But whatever I do, apart from the short cry (lyric poetry) and the short remark (journalism), must be in the form of notes. Mine is the talent of the cry or the *cahier*.

🖎 🖎

"My time will come," you say to yourself, but how can you know whether or not your time has not already come and gone? Perhaps one afternoon on the veranda in Panama, with the Barbadians' whetting their sickles on the hill below, the Chinese gardens green, the noise of breakers from beyond the hill, the crochet in your lap, and the cool room shuttered and the sheeted bed—perhaps that was your time. (But it was too early.) Or mornings in the sunny room in Boston, when the children cried loudly from the public school across the way, "A prairie is a *grassy* plain," and you sat on the low couch with your books and papers about you, happy and safe and calm: perhaps your time was then. (But you didn't see it at all.) Perhaps it has been spent, all spent, squandered out, in taking streetcars, drinking gin, smoking cigarettes—in connubial love, in thousands of books devoured by the eye, in eating, sewing, in suspicions, tears, jealousy, hatred, and fear. Perhaps it is now, on a dark day in October, in the bedroom where you sit with emptiness in your body and heart; beside the small fire, drying your hair—older, more tired, desperately silent, unhappily alone, with faith and daydreams (perhaps luckily) broken and disappearing, with the dreadful pain in your shoulder which presages dissolution, infection, and age. Perhaps this very instant is your time—pretty late—but still your own, your peculiar, your promised and presaged moment, out of all moments forever.

❧ ❧

The light on leaves in the evening looked as though it did not come from the sun, but from space itself, or from some element in a universe so distant from our own that it must be felt, never seen, and never named.

𝄢 𝄢

X said, "I think that at least four or five times a year, when people least expect it, drums should start in beating and the signal for a general saturnalia be given. While someone is out in a boat fishing, or alone in a room, or at an office desk, or washing up the breakfast dishes. Then all bets would be off, everyone would disappear into the crowd and forget and be forgotten, do what they please, and when everything was over, come back home completely satiated and without remorse."

It would take a generation to disabuse people of the idea that they could not *really* lay down their tools and go off on a singing-while-they-sway orgiastic time. Whole sections of the population would give thought to what they were going to wear to the general orgy, and whole sections would worry about how much the bender would cost. And as for the guilt: whole herds of scapegoats would swim in blood before the general sense of guilt could be washed away.

𝄢 𝄢

Long continued pain reduces one to the state of a bluster-ing child, or exacerbates one into an arrogant tyrant. Either "I can't bear this; help me" (with tears); or "I'm bearing this and don't you for a moment forget it."

𝄢 𝄢

October light has more time in it than any other. The day says "late" with its light, as summer mornings say "early" with theirs.

It is a day for everything. The trees in the little park are dry and brown because they have not been planted deeply; under them women in careful costumes sit and read, or talk to one another. The elevated train reverberates on its rails, and children have built a fire in the lot where they have not yet put up an apartment—the smoke drifts a long way, as clearly defined as the sound. Smoke drifts from the chimneys of the tenements—not much smoke—as from a poor fire, but from the apartment buildings decorated with crenellations a steady blue stream goes out sideways into the air. Little figures of men on steel work, streets away, sometimes come into view; the booms of derricks hold cables at clear angles, slender as threads. Light falls through the windows of empty apartments and lies on the floor marking the empty rooms into rectangles. The light falls against the leaves of plants, upright in the pots, and upon the lemon and tomato in the fruit dish, and upon the faded and dusty chintz of a chair that has worn through a summer.

I am older now than in any October before.

≰ ≰

"Literary friendships are a poisoned bowl," Yeats says in one of his later books. . . . Outwardly and really somewhat scornful of literary wowsers as they pretend to be, they yet cater to them, flatter them, join up with them. (L. Untermeyer goes on visits to Allen and then writes a review of the poems, the substance of which A. has probably dictated to him word for word; L. accepts invitations to P.E.N. club dinners, along with Pearl Buck and Genevieve Taggard. —Genevieve has done this sort of thing for years, so that no one can blame her for it; she knows her technique and uses it openly, at least, to gain her ends.)

My decision that I, too, must go to the P.E.N. dinner looking as regal as possible is, of course, a childish and ignoble idea. My life and hopes cannot be in that direction. So I'll turn it down. The world is not for me and can never be— I have not been trained to it and my approach to it is too easy, too false. I can assume too cleverly all the ignoble trappings that others assume with effort, and by the fey lightness and ease of my assumptions I am self-mocked and self-betrayed. No: all that is not mine and is not for me. But I must fear and desire it less. I must hate it less. I must learn to observe and judge, and forget to blame.

🙚 🙚

How pleasant offices are—even pleasanter than rooms in houses, on an autumn day like this. They are clean, well-lighted (thoroughly well lighted, so that melancholy cannot breed in the shadows between lamps); they have compatible chairs, books and papers, cigarette smoke, the sound of voices and of doors opening and shutting, clear gleaming dark linoleum floors. I come home and miss something in this room where I sit all day, now that winter is beginning. It is my room, my basis. But how lonely, how melancholy, at five o'clock, when taxis outside on Lexington Avenue hollowly sound their horns and streetcars grind by with that hysterical zoom. —Perhaps one could write in an office, people outside to touch and talk to—the electric light calmly suffusing the ceiling. Perhaps there alone an American artist may feel a tradition behind him and a culture backing him!

ɞ ɞ

I have learned a sonata by Mozart, written four pieces of criticism and a story. I have a new fountain pen and my hair has grown an inch. I have read Jane Carlyle's letters, two lives of Carlyle, Saintsbury's *Matthew Arnold* (Saintsbury died this month: also Galsworthy, that purveyor of sweetened liberal fiction to the English upper classes. Also Sara Teasdale). I saw Obey's *Lucrèce:* thought it very fine. Zabel was here at Christmas time: H. Monroe to dinner a week ago. Bought O. Sitwell's *Writers of Content.* Re-reading his *Discursions.* Reading Johnson's *Lives of the Poets.* Now know a great deal about Carlyle; Naples; something of Brahms' B Minor Capriccio. E. Wilson frequently to dinner. Party at J. Mosher's. Party at Slater Brown's. Frequently tormented by fears and loneliness at night.

Last night I woke and remembered the smooth architecture of clubs, good homes, fine shops, across the threshold of which I have never set foot nor shall ever set foot. I realized the sense of security in *place,* almost in life, that these outward symbols must give to those who frequent them. It is simple, at four in the morning, to feel an outcast. And is it to the imaginative that such feeling comes full force? Does the stenographer feel rootless because she has never dined at the Plaza or bought her clothes at Jay Thorpe's?—a quite different idea than snobbishness. The feeling arises from an imaginative grasp of what *these things must stand for,* the comfort they must give to those who just miss taking them as a matter of course. Even to anyone bred straight into them, they must give some solidity, no matter how matter of course they have become.

🖝 🖝

A journal concerned with the political scene, however well written and venomous, soon palls. What is staler than old politics? It is like walking over old furnace cinders to read what once was news of political chicanery or change.

🖝 🖝

That winter of her depression, a small round camera eye opened and shut in her memory and suddenly a scene would be disclosed with terrific clarity: she reassembled, in a flash, a scene complete to the kind of shadows on the ground and the kind of weather in the sky.

🖝 🖝

I thought again of the miracle of ornament: why did mankind throw up moldings and arabesques and intricate forms in wood and stone? Why was not all this creative impulse expended upon poetry (the heart's cry), speculation (the mind's search), or the pastime of story-telling alone? It was because the *hand* had to cry out as well as the heart.

🙠 🙠

The excessive boredom and even unhappiness that used to assail me on country journeys with R. can now be experienced, elucidated, as the landscape, the sounds, the light, giving me a clear, unpremeditated, unclouded-by-sentiment-or-passion-or-nonsense look, and expecting (and not, for the dullest of reasons, getting) a clear look back.

POEM IN PROSE

I turned from side to side, from image to image, to put you
    down,
All to no purpose; for you the rhymes would not ring—
Not for you, beautiful and ridiculous, as are always the true
    inheritors of love,
The bearers; their strong hair moulded to their foreheads as
    though by the pressure of hands.
It is you that must sound in me secretly for the little time
    before my mind, schooled in desperate esteem, forgets you—
And it is my virtue that I cannot give you out,
That you are absorbed into my strength, my mettle,
That in me you are matched, and that it is silence which comes
    from us.

Sometime I must do real justice to the American gentility of the Holdens: the uncle who lived in the country with his shrewish wife and played ping-pong and collected stamps; the two sisters with a girl-friend (a strong-minded and dictatorial girl-friend) apiece; the mother's sisters, satellites of her, who had the money; a brother no one ever saw, kept way off up in the country somewhere (what was the matter with him, I wonder?). They (the mother and aunts) had in a Swedish masseuse one winter to massage them all, and she told me strange tales of sororal jealousy. —The Whistlers, the George Washington clock and plates, the good, solid, perfectly tasteless food, the passion for glass and china (fostered by a Jewish woman with a Spanish shop, who spent her life fostering glass-and-china-and-barber's-basins-(brass)-and-tooled-leather-and-hand-woven-linen passions in members of the bourgeoisie). The fine bindings in the library, the pages uncut. The Garden Club. Marion's boat-house (fixed up so charmingly with Spanish and Italian and Early American junk, as above). Clock-golf. The tennis court that nobody ever used. The rather dotty butler Mrs. H. was frightened of. —They were all frightened of something, I never could make out what.

᚜ ᚜

THOREAU'S JOURNAL: FEBRUARY 5TH, 1855
"In a journal it is important in a few words to describe the weather, or character of the day, as it affects our feelings. That which was so important at the time cannot be unimportant to remember."

The wind blew; footsteps came to the side door; it was now late autumn: all the magnificent dahlias had wilted down from their props and the maple tree on the lawn was as bare as your hand. . . . The sunlight was so strong, on bright days, that it cast strong shadows all through the house; you could tell the time of day and the season of the year from the way the shadow slanted back from table and chair legs, just as easily as from the shadows of objects out of doors. . . .

Under the thin, pale, delicate light, the rocky pastures rose gently against the sky. Long looked upon by solitude. Solitude had drained into the ground, like the sun and rain. Chips of mica glistened in the rocks.
"It looks like rain."

The room full of woodsmoke. The *waiting* rain-gray sky
Shots in the woods—the cicadas
A scene: first color, then design—then light and shade . . .

Santayana's classic world—the people of Chekhov "seen against the sky": this is what I knew in childhood and had no word for: this is "the light falling down through the universe," the look and feeling of which has haunted me for so long—

The long late light, in childhood. Autumn desolation. The windy raw autumn afternoon, with light and dark alternating over the hills and fields, and great sweeps of gray cloud giving the light its silence, its feeling of tears, of sorrow, of desperation. The light that would return, over a lifetime of autumns . . . At a certain hour, a look of terrible mystery and silence . . .

At first, it was, perhaps, all that mankind had to delight in (above their cruder delights)—the only thing that approximated art, as we know it: these changes of light that the day brings. Afternoon, instead of a Tintoretto. Evening, instead of Brahms or Debussy or (most especially) Mozart.

Thank God, I shall be dead when, in a brave new world, both the light and the art are forgotten!

She did not like books with no weather in them. Or paintings in which the objects cast no shadows . . .

❧ ❧

And what of that feeling of unearthly splendor, of great promise, terrible delight, at some seasons of the year? Or the excitement which came with early darkness, and cold; or with summer heat, letting down torrents of brilliant summer light, that had to be shut out of the houses? This look and sound of promise fled through the town with the trains, and with the ripples on the river. "Some day! Some day!" it said.

This promise could be referred to nothing. The child lives in a region it knows nothing about. So that whatever memory of childhood remains is stable and perfect. It cannot be judged and it can never disappear. Memory has it inexplicably, and will have it forever. These things have been actually "learned by heart."

❧ ❧

View from my window: 70 Morningside Drive

A long view over roofs, that includes bridges, churches, hospitals, elevated trains, gas tanks, apartment houses, chimneys, and trees (*but not the streets themselves*) is, perhaps, important to the imagination because, seen from a height, all these things look like *toys,* and that, in some way, is important to us; that kind of sight.

In reality, how many clouds there are that blow over the city, that no one ever sees!

I had become actually angry with the trees below my window, because they remained all twigs, even in the second week in April, and one morning it seemed that I could see them bud under my very eyes and I wanted to slow up the process, then.

The trees, in young new leaves, *move,* as they never did in winter. I remember distinctly how still and stiff they were. But now, *not only the leaves,* the whole tree moves, bends, liquifies, *waves* from side to side. As though the very roots had loosened.

The dreadful thing about north rooms: not that there is no sunlight in them now, but that there has never been sun in them . . . like the minds of stupid people: that have been stupid from the beginning and will be stupid forever.

I have always tended to settle myself into unfriendly surroundings, and then allow myself to be bothered by them. —Must get over this.

Edward Hopper's "A Room in Brooklyn." A room my heart yearns to: uncurtained, hardly furnished, with a view over roofs. A clean bed, a bookcase, a kitchen, a calm mind, one or two half-empty rooms—all my life wants to achieve, and I have not yet achieved it. —I have tried too hard for the wrong things. If I would concentrate on getting the spare room, I could have it almost at once. . . . I must have it.

↜ ↜

Today it seemed as though nothing would ever happen again. Saw my real, half-withered, silly face in a shop mirror on the street, under the bald light of an evening shower, and shuddered. The woman who died without producing an *oeuvre*. The woman who ran away.

The faithlessness and falsehoods of one you love can wound you: the stupidities of one you do not love cause nothing but anger and annoyance. —This is a remark you have said to yourself but seldom, if ever, heard.

I felt that his soul was like a small rectangular piece of wood or bone: a domino: hard: one inch long and a half inch wide, residing in the unmeasured depth of what we all possess.

But how beautiful he would have been, if he had had a "good heart"! How life would have flowered, with him! But he *was* the bad heart. The disguised bad heart was the blood in his veins. A possession of evil.

Stupidity *always* accompanies evil. Or evil, stupidity.

The presence, in an otherwise strange face, of the nose of a person you once loved.

A woman so dry, so ugly, so severe, that it seemed impossible that she had been generated by the sexual act.

Is it true that lack of regular sexual intercourse produces in a woman idleness and dryness? Are we like gardens, that must be continually hoed and scratched and (to invert the figure) weeded?

The old ladies, condemned to feed upon each other.

The lack of good restaurants, the frightful collection of old female wrecks, in the uptown streets.

The sad, large, ugly ears of the old.

The woman's hair was so importantly waved and curled and burnished and combed, that her face, beneath it, and in contrast to it, gave the exact effect of a zero.

    ϟ ϟ

A bourgeois pastime: distrusting and spying on the servants. When I got to Provincetown this summer Betty and Edmund were indulging in a regular orgy of suspicions directed toward Hattie. Ed not so much, of course, but Betty was up in indignation to her chin. And Hattie, as far as I could see, was a devoted and honest woman.

The woman behind me on the bus with the terrible, frigid upper-class accent, carrying on because my long hair no doubt impressed and unnerved her, and she thought she had an audience.

(At Columbus Circle) "My memories of this goes back to my *infancy*: I used to cross it to take my music lesson when I was eight years old."

"When I was ten, when we came back from Europe, we stayed there."

"All my life seems to fall into definite sections: there was my life with father and mother and then with mother, and when that was over it was as though a book was closed. Does your life seem like that?" (To her husband, who didn't respond much to the extremely quiet and deft theatrics. Husband: "I never thought of it.")

"New York is a series of villages, like London, isn't it?"

Then she got off onto bicycle paths on Riverside Drive; and her child (I'm sure she calls him "my small son") that I couldn't see and hadn't heard peep up to that time asked, "Where are we going, Mother?" "Up Riverside," she said, about five times, coldly and without the slightest human variation in her voice.

That accent: those adjectives. "And now John has eight dogs on his hands that have to be treated like human beings and he is rapidly going mad. Sweet idea, isn't it?"

I thought of a great many things, like murder, as I staggered off the bus. Of course she was pitiable: frozen and somehow afraid, or she wouldn't have had to show off like that. But she had the man and the child in absolute control. Complete. Father and mother had certainly done a good job of it, in her case.

Is it father-cum-mother-cum-the-class? It's certainly not the class *alone* that produces these people. But I must admit for a moment I blamed it all on the class. But she was born frozen, in any class.

NEW MOON

Cruel time-servers, here is the crescent moon,
Curved right to left in the sky, facing planets attendant.

Over the houses, leaned in the silent air,
Purest along the edge of darkness infinite.

Under it, men return from the office and factory,
From the little store at the corner of Eighty-eighth Street.

On the gnawed snow, or under the breezes of autumn,
With hope and fear in their hearts, and their arms full of
    groceries.

Above the trim suit, above the flesh starved or satiate,
Above the set hair, above the machines in the beauty-shops;

Above the young men, thinking the popular song;
Above the children, who now in the dusk go wild.

Crescent, horn, cusp, above the clinics, the lodgings,
Sweet curve, sweet light, new thin moon, now purely at ease,
Above the old, going home to their deafness, their madness,
Their cancer, age, ugliness, pain, diabetes.

❦ ❦

A thousand kindnesses do not make up for a thousand
blows.

The lechery of men of middle age is as hard as a stone.

They kiss as though they threw their faces against one; they do not wait and draw in passion as young men do; they strike out at a woman in a kind of frenzy, give embraces in a cold scuffle. They are afraid of being pitiful themselves, so they cannot give out that pity which a woman waits for in any embrace. They make love usually when they are drunk. They speak of golf, their sons and daughters, sometimes of their wives, in the intervals of throwing against a woman that hard face, those cold eyes, those hands tightened up like fists, that dreadful, cold, half-opened mouth with its licking tongue—

In their cage, at evening in the zoo, one hippopotamus, with his great low hanging ponderous face, nuzzled the side of another. What if tenderness should be lost everywhere else, and left only in these creatures?

❦ ❦

———— sat in the chair and said, "I'm in fine physical shape," and told me about the sanitarium. He had worked in the carpenter shop where both men and women patients worked together, and one girl sang continually, and a man said to him, "Rather vocal this morning, isn't it?" —He was completely through with Dr. ————. "I don't believe in this psychiatry business at all any more. I went to Dr. ———— and he sat there saying, 'Yes, Yes' sucking on his pipe. 'Yes, yes' and he told me I should go away for a while. Business worries. I was worried about the office."

And as he said all this, his eyes looked drunk, although he no longer drinks, so it must be Luminol that he takes in the day as well as at night. And he kept popping his index finger in and out of his mouth: a new *tic*; he never did that before. —At dinner he spoke of the people who hung about old Mrs. ———— who was 76 and loved celebrities. One boy in particular: "a degenerate if there ever was one: all the things a man should not be." —He thought Santayana's philosophy essentially evil: he has heard that S. is a homosexual.

How clear these symptoms stand forth, to anyone who knows how they fit together: how unsafe it is to be without insight into your own case! He thought he had me thoroughly fooled as to the real trouble, and each gesture told me what was really the matter.

ᚷ ᚷ

Telephone conversations of the normal young academicians. They run on about nothing—visits; what Aunt Mary did; whether the deaf child should go to a private school (the deafness is called, of course, "a handicap"); the weather. They (the academicians) are gentle, kind, and rather flattering, in a toneless way. They never really laugh, make jokes, talk about food, or swear.

ᚷ ᚷ

The woman beside me on the Amsterdam Avenue bus was reading a letter, and I glanced toward it. "Dearest Kit," it began. I did not look at her until I left (the letter seemed to be from a sailor who was going through the Panama Canal), but when I did look, I saw that she was no ordinary woman, but a real beauty, under the cheap hat and bad hair-curl, and above the scroungy fur of her coat. Her eyelashes were as thick as a hedge, and her eyes the most extraordinary blue; she had fine skin and a mouth fit for Isolde. So there is love for beauty still going on, I thought.

❦ ❦

To understand: not to fear: not to hate: not to envy. —All that is easy; but all at once, beyond my will, I find myself hating the childish old, in their uniform getups (who have not lived) and the childish informed (with their nasty hatreds) who have never "wrung the last drop of the slave from their soul."

❦ ❦

In youth only one thing, one attribute, is needed to make us overlook, in the beloved, the lack or the distortion of all the rest (and that attribute is usually physical beauty). In maturity one attribute, even if it be physical beauty, is not enough to make us overlook the lack of a good heart, a good mind, fibre in the temperament, etc., etc. We get so that we do not want even that one: we are content, as we love it, to keep away from it. But at no age does our love (or should not) for the single gift, when present in another, really cease.

When we have not come into ourselves we say, in solitude: "No one loves me; I am alone." When we have chosen solitude, we say: "Thank God, I am alone!"

First, that it should be romantic, exciting; then, that it

should be bearable; and at last, that it should be understandable! These are the stages which we go through, in forming our desires concerning life.

For two years I have gathered up learning and philosophy, and now I find I have no life to use them on!

⇜ ⇜

One of the few rewards of a hard struggle with critical values and nonsense and pomposity in general is, that after long years of it, one is always, and almost automatically, right: the chance of being taken in not only dwindles, but completely vanishes. (This on the occasion of C. Fadiman's admitting that, in 1932, he was wrong about C. Morgan's *The Fountain*. I was right about C. Morgan's *The Fountain*, but *at the time*, I thought I might merely be the victim of mean-spirited thinking; I did not trust my own judgment thoroughly. —I trust it implicitly now.)

"I have done some living; I now read a great deal."

Reading *Crime and Punishment* and Turgenev. The Isabel Hapgood translations of Turgenev are so horrible that they should be destroyed *in toto*. Did no one ever say, when they appeared, how horrible they are? Did this sort of translation get by in the early 20th century, and no one said a word!

Really understood *C & P* for the first time.

Turgenev's *Virgin Soil* the finest analysis of the hysterical revolutionary I have ever seen. His analysis of the only kind of ruler Russia will follow—a saint or demi-god—also remarkable. What beauty—and kept from me for years by that damned Isabel Hapgood. The effects of light and shadow on the scene as beautiful as anything I have ever read, even in Thoreau or Chekhov.

Let me never forget James' beautiful, understanding, touching articles on George Sand. Even the earliest, 1897, is enchanting, and the latest one, written in 1914, carries over the same insight and sympathy. These pieces of criticism have endeared James to me as nothing else of his, and because my sympathy was completely touched, I recognized some of James' excellences of style, never recognized so completely before: his success with large figures of comparison; his essentially literary, but nevertheless colloquially lightened language—he had the true Yankee-Irish (more Irish than Yankee, but an amalgam of both) gift for the use of the common word and the idiom of common speech. Toward the last, he tended to abjure these colloquialisms; he set them off, like bad or ill-dressed children, with quotation marks. They were absorbed into, and used rightly in, the earlier Jamesian style.

(Having seen a page of Henry James' corrected manuscript): Dear God, why does anyone *write*! Even for him, it didn't come out well, the first time. And those books and books. A *hero*.

List of books on my shelves, before they are packed and dispersed for the summer. A list of this sort, put down from time to time, may identify and color the memory of a period of time, spent in a certain way. I wish I had put down other such lists, during my past career.

Prokosch and Morgan—Introduction to German
Shakespeare—Histories and Poems
                —Tragedies
Yeats—Wheels and Butterflies
Pascal—Pensées (introduction by Eliot)
Fowler—Modern English Usage
Valéry—Morceaux Choisis
Life of Chekhov (in Russian)
    (Edmund's gift: many photographs)
Salvaneschi—Brevario della Felicità
    (bought as Italian reader in Palermo)
Molière/J.B. Poquelin—Comedies
Rilke, R. M.—Sonnets on Orpheus
Leopardi—Canti
Grandgent and Wilkins—Italian Grammar
Cocteau, J.—Portraits Souvenir
Burke, K.—Permanence and Change
Rilke, R. M.—Briefe an Seinen Verleger
Meynell, Viola—Follow Thy Fair Sun
Lucretius—De Rerum Natura
Dante—Inferno, Purgatorio, Paradiso
La Rochefoucauld. Refléxions, sentences, et maximes morales
Vauvenargues—Oeuvres choisies
Congreve—Plays
Auden and Garrett—The Poet's Tongue
Morand, P.—Rond-Point des Champs-Élysées
Coleridge—Selected Poetry and Prose
Isherwood, C.—The Last of Mr. Norris
Borchert, A.—Mozart
Yeats, W. B.—The Great Clock Tower
Colette—Duo
            —Textes Choisis
Gide, A.—Si le grain ne meurt
Colette—Mes Apprentissages

Macauley, R.—Personal Pleasures
Eliot, T. S.—Essays Ancient and Modern
        —Elizabethan Essays
        —Collected Poems
Spender, S.—Vienna
Renard, J.—Journal
Valéry, P.—Monsieur Teste
Bishop, J. P.—Minute Particulars
Warren, R. P.—Thirty-Six Poems
Rosenfeld, P.—Discoveries of a Music Critic
Baudelaire, C.—Flowers of Evil, trans. by Dillon and Millay
Matthiessen—The Achievement of T. S. Eliot
Douglas, N.—Old Calabria
Rilke, R. M.—Neue Gedichte
Das Kleine Buch der Tropen Wundern

❦ ❦

How preposterous, how unbearable is literature: reality
dished up in the phrase; men and women inflated out of
recognition by the noun, verb, adverb, adjective. "The willows
stood by the stream, their boles gray and pewter in the early
light." And under them stands a creature without pores in its
chin or growing hair or fingernails or teeth (unless they be
"discolored" or "beautiful"), and over them hangs "a moon
like a slice of melon" or "the million icy points of the stars."

The paper people in books, who have one agony to endure,
one set of toils to fight clear of, in their lives. Figures that
breathe print and the air of the paragraph and the page.
—One should set oneself the task, in full maturity, to fix on
paper the bizarre, disordered, ungainly, furtive, mixed ele-

ments in one's life, the opposite of the paper people—and the men and women in masks, halved queerly in their natures—the destiny which stands half in us, half about us, and is often in the hands of these split and equivocal beings. . . .

Why I could never be happy writing fiction: Because fiction, unless it is half poetry, is always a put up job on reality. Poetry gives reality freedom and meaning. . . .

11 *Back through plains*

🖎 🖎 Although a major achievement of our time has been the clinical proof that the letter killeth, while the spirit giveth life; that it is healthier to love than to hate; that maturity means responsibility; that the closed nature is the nature in which mania takes root; that if one refuses to go forward, one immediately starts to go back, this discovery has not been generally absorbed. Nostalgia, cruelty, and gloom are not so much the signs of the death of culture as they are of individual regression. The artist, as one Marxian critic has pointed out, does not function in a vacuum. Neither does he function out of a vacuum. Poetry is an activity of the spirit; its roots lie deep in the subconscious nature, and it withers if that nature is denied, neglected, or negated.

No amount of heroic action, no adherence to noble beliefs can release poetic expression to order. The dialectical play of the mind or the aggressive action of the body affect its functioning not at all. Its battles are fought in secret and, perhaps, "are never lost or won." The certain method of stilling poetic talent is to substitute an outer battle for an inner one. A poet emerges from a spiritual crisis strengthened and refreshed only if he has been strong enough to fight it through at all levels, and at the deepest first. One refusal to take up the gage thrown down by his own nature leaves the artist confused and maimed. And it is not one confrontation, but many, which must be dealt with and resolved. The first evasion throws the poet back into a lesser state of development which no show of bravado can conceal. "A change of heart" is the result of slow and difficult inner adjustments. A mere shift in allegiance, if it is not backed up by conflict genuinely resolved, produces, in the artist, as it produces in any one, confusion and insincerity. The two great poets of our time, Rilke and Yeats, because they fought their own battles on their own ground, became, first, mature men, and then mature artists. They drew to themselves more and more experience; their work never dried up at the source or bloated into empty orotundity. The later poetry of both is work based on simple expression, deep insight, and deep joy.

It is difficult to say what a woman poet should concern herself with as she grows older, because women who have produced an impressively bulky body of work are few. But is there any reason to believe that a woman's spiritual fibre is less sturdy than a man's? Is it not possible for a woman to come to terms with herself, if not with the world; to withdraw more and more, as time goes on, her own personality from her productions; to stop childish fears of death and eschew charming rebellions against facts?

KEPT

Time for the wood, the clay,
The trumpery dolls, the toys
Now to be put away:
We are not girls and boys.

What are these rags we twist
Our hearts upon, or clutch
Hard in the sweating fist?
They are not worth so much.

But we must keep such things
Till we at length begin
To feel our nerves their strings,
Their dust, our blood within.

The dreadful painted bisque
Becomes our very cheek.
A doll's heart, faint at risk,
Within our breast grows weak.

Our hand the doll's, our tongue.

Time for the pretty clay,
Time for the straw, the wood.
The playthings of the young
Get broken in the play,
Get broken, as they should.

In the late 30s, in a transitional period both of my outer circumstances and my central beliefs, I wrote a poem—"Zone"—which derives directly from emotional crisis, as, I feel, a lyric must. And I think that the poem's imagery manages to express, in concrete terms (the concrete terms which poetry demands), some reflection of those relentless universal laws under which we live—which we must not only accept but in some manner forgive—as well as the fact of the human courage and faith necessary to that acceptance.

ZONE

We have struck the regions wherein we are keel or reef.
The wind breaks over us,
And against high sharp angles almost splits into words,
And these are of fear or grief.

Like a ship, we have struck expected latitudes
Of the universe, in March.
Through one short segment's arch
Of the zodiac's round
We pass,
Thinking: Now we hear
What we heard last year,
And bear the wind's rude touch
And its ugly sound
Equally with so much
We have learned how to bear.

🙢 🙢

What makes a writer? Is it the love of, and devotion to, the actual act of writing that makes a writer? I should say, from my own experience, NO. Some of the most untalented people *adore* writing: some have elaborate set-ups for the ritual: enormous desks, boxes of various kinds of paper; paper clips; pencil-sharpeners; several sorts of pen; erasers, ink, and what-not. In the midst of all this they sit and write interminably. I suppose they *could* be called writers; but they should not be.

Is it intellectual power? Yes, I suppose so: of a kind. But it is sometimes the kind of intellect that is not fitted to pass examinations. It need not include, for example, the kind of photographic memory that produces a school career of straight A's. It is certainly not intellectual power functioning in an abstract way.

A writer's power is based on what we have come to call *talent*, which the dictionary describes first off as "a special natural ability or aptitude." Later on in this definition, talent is described as a *gift*. It is as a gift that I prefer to think of it. The ancients personified the giver of the gift as the Muse—or the Muses: the Daughters of Memory. The French use the word *souffle* figuratively for what passes between the Muse and the artist or writer—*le souffle du génie*—the breath of inspiration; and any writer worth his salt has felt this breath. It comes and goes; it cannot be forced and it can very rarely be summoned up by the conscious will.

The writer's gift usually manifests itself fairly early. The adolescent writer-to-be finds himself or herself *compelled* to write. These young people also are usually voracious readers. First they read everything that comes to hand; soon they find themselves seeking out what they feel to be *theirs*. In spite of all obstacles, they track down what they feel to be their own: from all periods of written literature, and often in several languages. *Words* are their passion; they intoxicate themselves with words. And almost immediately they begin to find their own idiosyncratic rhythm and pulse, to which the words may be fitted. They imitate others, naturally. But what they are looking for is their own voice and their own words. So, very naturally, they come upon the writer's second necessity: the mastering of technique. That battle never ends.

Talent and technique: the basic needs of a writer. For, as the talent, the gift, grows, it begins to absorb the other more usually human attributes. It draws intuition, intellect, curiosity, observation to itself; and it begins to absorb emotion as well. For a writer's power is based not upon his intellect so much as upon his intuition and his emotions. All art, in spite of the struggles of some critics to prove otherwise, is based on emotion and projects emotion.

The process by which emotion is translated into a pattern of words is unknowable. The emotion must be strong enough not only to produce the initial creative impulse, but to prefigure, in part, the structure of the poem as a whole. Not everything is "given," but enough of the design should come through to determine the poem's shape, direction and speed. The rest must be filled in by the conscious mind, which, ideally, knows all the artful devices of language.

The gift comes and goes. As W. H. Auden remarked, a poet can never be certain, after writing one poem, that he will ever be able to write another. Training and experience can never be completely counted on; the "breath," the "inspiration" may be gone forever. All one can do is try to remain "open" and hope to remain sincere. Openness and sincerity will protect the poet from giving in to fits of temper; from small emotions with which poetry should not, and cannot deal; as well as from imitations of himself or others. The interval between poems, as poets have testified down the ages, is a lonely time. But then, if the poet is lucky and in a state of grace, a new emotion forms, and a new poem begins, and all is, for the moment, well.

Apprenticeship, a period of full flowering, and a gradual decline in creative energy—the usual progress of a lyric poet who does not force or falsify his gifts.

🙦 🙦

You can think of me spending days in perfectly unprofitable idleness. Perhaps I can write poetry again, I think, if the timetable can be completely upset for a time. So I read cookbooks and play the music I knew as a child, and try to raise petunias and morning glories in the windows. (Trivial pastimes; but so many people are making an inhuman job of being "useful" and "serious.")

Music in those days belonged to its own time and place. No one today can remember with the same nostalgia (my generation is the last to remember) the sound of music on the water (voices and a mandolin or guitar); of band concerts in town squares or in Army parade grounds, in the twilight or early evening, with a string of lights in the distance marking the line of the bay; or under trees in what was actually, then, a romantic "gloaming." How poignant the sound of piano music, played however inexpertly, along some city street; or even, in those days, when every child was exposed to piano lessons, and the "upright" in the parlor was a sign of respectability and some slight edge of affluence, along some suburban road, or some half-country lane! Laforgue has caught the effect at the moment, I suppose in the 80s, when it was most usual—

"*Pianos, pianos, dans les quartiers aisés.*"

TO BE SUNG ON THE WATER

Beautiful, my delight,
Pass, as we pass the wave.
Pass, as the mottled night
Leaves what it cannot save,
Scattering dark and bright.

Beautiful, pass and be
Less than the guiltless shade
To which our vows were said;
Less than the sound of the oar
To which our vows were made,—
Less than the sound of its blade
Dipping the stream once more.

It is not only the pianos that have vanished (the sound of the pianos along the streets in spring evenings when the windows were opened) but the world in which they sounded, and the young ears that they sounded for. I shall never forget how beautiful they were, or what they meant to me. And when I say that their world has vanished, I mean it poignantly: the slant of light over the shabby streets of that time. Totally shabby American streets with no shine or *chic* in them, only a few doorsteps, lamp-posts, carriage (wagon) wheels (and the sound that tired horses' feet used to make, when the horses shifted them), trees, and lighted windows—and the tireless scales, like grain flowing from the hand, or the bad pieces those children used to play.

🙋 🙋

My daughter is living with me again. Maidie has a room at the back, where her piano is, so we don't annoy each other too much. It is, I'll admit, a temptation to go in and play her accompaniments for her, when she is working, and I should be.

M., SINGING

Now, innocent, within the deep
Night of all things you turn the key,
Unloosing what we know in sleep.
In your fresh voice they cry aloud
Those beings without heart or name.

Those creatures both corrupt and proud,
Upon the melancholy words
And in the music's subtlety,
Leave the long harvest which they reap
In the sunk land of dust and flame
And move to space beneath our sky.

I am a terrible accompanist, I may add, especially for Strauss and Debussy songs which have eight or nine sharps or flats, and interpolated measures in 5/4 time. But it is more fun than writing. I sometimes think that anything is more fun than literary composition. . . .

Life is to be enjoyed, and if it is not, it makes people ill in one way or another. —Have you ever read Jung's book on this subject? It is his latest one, I can't remember the title. But in it the sensitive doctor proves that joy can't be circumvented. If the mind takes over too much, the body slaps back in the form of symptoms. —It is dreadful to think of all the energy mankind expends in the effort to wipe out, or negate, joy.

I have always found that the best way of keeping from going mad is to *let* yourself have some fun. Not just *have* a good time, but *let* yourself have one. "Having a good time" is a phrase that has always puzzled me, from childhood on. On my birthday I was "given" a "good time," occasionally: roller-coasters and unlimited candy and soda and steamed clams and sand-digging, and I always wondered, the next day, whether it had been "a good time": it just seemed like roller-coasters and unlimited candy, etc., etc.

The difficulty was, in my childhood, that I expected everything to mean something. . . .

12 Back along love

ﾚ ﾚ   The strongly poignant (and unexpectedly so) set of feelings set up, over the weekend, by my rereading of "the packet of letters": Raymond's letters and cables to me in the summer of 1933 (the love letters) and a few of his subsequent letters, after the separation (the playing-like-a-trout or hate letters!). After I read a few of mine to him, in that 1933 summer, a whole complex of suffering came back.

PACKET OF LETTERS

In the shut drawer, even now, they rave and grieve—
To be approached at times with the frightened tear;

Their cold to be drawn away from, as one, at nightfall,
Draws the cloak closer against the cold of the marsh.

There, there, the thugs of the heart did murder.
There, still in murderers' guise, two stand embraced,
    embalmed.

I thought that this complex of feelings had vanished forever, long ago; and it had! The extraordinary thing about
the revived experience was its power to bring back the moments in time, in place—the vignettes of pain, placed in a
series of settings. Also the same sense of being *trapped*—of
being used, of being made an *object*. This nightmare effect
stayed with me for about a day and a night—in which I re-
lived the whole set of emotions, felt from that April through
that September.

(That year, from time to time, she was haunted by what
now seemed the wasted years of her marriage: the time lost in
jealousy, anger, tension, alcohol. What could she not have
done, given a normal life and a normal husband! Given some
economic freedom, some hard hand over her, some impulsion
to work!

(And yet, what had she missed, she would think again, save
happiness and productivity? She had lived through all the
possible range of nerves, fear, and unquiet, and she had
stiffened herself into a mould of love as perhaps no one else
had stiffened, before or since. What could she have known
otherwise? What could she have seen (for now she knew
happiness did not crown the bough, however perfect the

partner)? What was this she had missed that she had per-
suaded herself she should have had? After all, she had had
something and that is all anyone alive gets: something. And
that something is never a real waste or loss.)

But on the second morning I came out of it all with a
perfectly cool and contemporary reaction: it was all too *boring*
to review any longer, in memory; or to re-feel, in life.

❦ ❦

TO TAKE LEAVE

Now, look here, my fine pair, widely known as Sorrow and
Romantic Attachment, I have entertained the thought of you
over a long period of years. I have enjoyed you as a delight
and endured you as a burden. I have summered and wintered
you, and I have given you the unmistakable advantages of
both penury and travel. Because of me you have been exposed to cities whose public splendor is equalled by their private squalor, and you have also experienced the close confines
of suburbs whose scene and population have the unrewarding
tone and texture of stale bread. I have had your good, not to
say your education, at heart.

I have dragged you far south and quartered you in houses
triply sealed against the sun, in a country of cracked church
bells, oranges, lemons, mimosa, and cinerarias, where the
honey has a bitter taste and the coffee smells of chloroform.
Together we have taken refuge from the blinding streets in
museums, where we were bored by small funerary objects,

astounded by great sprays of coral rooted in bronze helmets, and pleased by various forms of painting and sculpture. We have listened to fountains in gardens. We have sat, long Sunday afternoons, in the parlors of third-class hotels, among the stopped clocks and the cracked ormolu. With breast-high furniture all about us, we have heard the punctual after-dinner clatter of thick dishes echo against the steep, stained courts of *pensions*; in the morning we have stumbled over the slattern mop and pail; at night we have turned to sleep in rooms soaked through and through with the pattern of bad wallpaper. Together we have experienced the misery of things and the grandeur of nature (for volcanoes, oceans, and mountain passes have not been unknown to us).

Because of you, my horrid twain, and dogged by you every inch of the way, I have walked through hot or rainy streets and driven miles in various broken-down vehicles to post and telegraph offices; I have inquired daily for mail at little grilles that penned in surly natives of several countries; I have, each morning, met the old men and women, the old ashtrays and the old newspapers in the waiting-rooms of tourist bureaus. In all weathers, in all climates, in railway stations and on wharves, you have touched my sympathies and exacerbated my nerves. With the pair of you at my elbow, I have sat up all night writing letters and wept all day, waiting to receive them. Faced with 1880 stucco façades, preserved in the white glare of Mediterranean sunlight (which has many of the preservative qualities of formaldehyde), or surrounded by damp mountain airs and the huts and hay barns of simple cowherds, things have been much the same between us.

Whether I ate off the grass or bare boards or my lap or the hot or cold plates on restaurant tables, I was invariably conscious of your presence. Standing on bridges, leaning over balustrades, at the grocer's, the library, the work table, the hairdresser's, I could not escape you. Bands played in the open square, piano music fell down from high open windows, boats lowed at night on the river, trains whistled half a township away, awaking the nostalgia and the yearning so dear to you. None of us heard these sounds alone.

It is your persistence, as well as your ubiquity, that has compelled me to take my present stand. Landmarks disappeared and towers grew up out of excavations, but nothing made any difference to you. Styles changed. The human race acquired new habits, new means of transportation, new catchwords, and new rulers. Walls that stood bare at our first meeting now rise clothed in ivy; several new blights have wiped out several different varieties of trees. Summers have increased in heat and winters in cold. What with birth and death, since we three came together, a very nearly new set of people now inhabit the globe.

We can't go on like this any longer, my friends and far-too-constant companions. I sometimes feel that you or I, or possibly the three of us in combination, are obstructing the stream of progress. Our common advantages haven't done us much good. To continue to live with you would, in my present opinion, dampen my enthusiasms and blunt my initiative to an extent exceeding their present dampness and bluntness. I no longer wish to spend another moment of time wondering, in the watches of the night, whether the pair of you will be pleasant, accountable, and feasible tomorrow, as you were unfeasible, unpleasant, and unaccountable yesterday. The intense pleasures of anxiety, as time passes, attract me less and less. Plans for your liquidation occupy me more and more. This is a short speech to take leave.

So goodbye, grief. Goodbye, love.

When it is over, you say to yourself: "Never possibly can I feel that way again." It is like a wild beast in the heart, that turns its prey over slowly, seeking the soft places, the tender places between bone and bone, the yielding muscle and soft flesh, wherein the teeth may sink. It is at once the victim and the beast. Quietly they lie together, on fresh grass, and again enter the slow struggle, the torture beyond feeling. The dead yet living victim is turned; the eater seeks slowly, passionately, the next place in which to set its fang. The wounds are made but do not bleed.

Just afterward, a mood of pity descends on the freshly punished spirit. Everything in the world becomes piteous, and not a sound or sight can escape from the love wrapped in fog and obscurity: secret to itself. Those nearest the heart drain off the first pity. How lovely they are, and how vulnerable! Their flesh, their very being, draws out the misty love like a thread: over and over it wraps them round. Today they live; their hair seems exquisitely clean and lies bright on their foreheads. They are young. Their bodies and their wishes will come to nothing. It is our purpose to love them; yet the thread continues to wrap them round until they live inside a cocoon of this soft emotion which is part dread.

They cannot see nor hear nor feel the love that pours out to them. Soft and delicate as fright in the dark, over and around them it goes. They sink into it. The heart pulls them down. "Forgive me; forgive me," the heart says, "you are beautiful and you will die. You are not really young, happy, or beautiful. You are appearance; you change as I love you. This moment turns and changes, and you also change. Goodbye, goodbye," says the heart, taking its sombre, its delicate, its tender leave. "I am all around you; you cannot really hear me, for I am one field, one wood, one acre too far away. The children toss the ball, but it is too dark to see it any longer. Farewell, farewell."

13 Back through noon

🖎 🖎   I'm really very proud of myself that I've managed to do "journalism" all these years. I'm a professional: I can turn it out. But I'm such a slow writer, and there's no one lazier than I. No one. I hate every minute of it.

First I read, then I take notes—sometimes too many—on yards of yellow foolscap; then I write a first draft, then a second. But I know now that it's possible. I remember, in the beginning, sitting at that desk with the tears pouring down my face trying to write a notice. Edmund Wilson would pace behind me and exhort me to go on. He taught me a great deal, at a period when I needed a teacher.

(Edmund speaks of Emerson's lack of real intellectual

power: the essays are flashes, held together by no structure of "fundamental brainwork." And the thought struck me that I should take notes happily all my life, not ever troubling to put them into form. I am a woman, and "fundamental brainwork," the building of logical structures, the abstractions, the condensations, the comparisons, the reasonings, *are not expected of me*. But it is only when I am making at least an imitation of such a structure that I am really happy. It is only when the notes fall into form, when the sentences make *at least the sound of style*, that my interest really holds.)

ᔥ ᔥ

3 SEPTEMBER 1962

I'm *mapping out* the woman bards lecture that Bennington has asked me to give. Not a cliché.

5 SEPTEMBER 1962

I am at last covering paper, in the matter of the women's poetry piece, and I bought a red pencil, yesterday, with which to make *loops*. A paperback, *Women in Antiquity*, by a learned Cambridge scholar (Charles Seltman) is giving me the dope on pre-history, Egypt, and Greece. Did Diotima exist? etc., etc. . . . I'm struggling against every kind of *idée reçue*, believe me. And Simone de Beauvoir is a formidable opponent. . . .

8 SEPTEMBER 1962

I am surrounded by pine-needles, mushrooms, and lovely late flowers. The actual writing of the piece will begin on Monday.

14 September 1962

I now have six fairly permanently blackened pages. It all ebbs and flows. But I'm out of Simone de B.'s clutches.

18 September 1962

The piece is slowly getting into form—quite different than originally planned.

19 September 1962

Only three or four full days of work left. The piece is advancing, but it keeps changing under the pen. V. strange. I may end up with just a bunch of detached sentences.

27 September 1962

—Odds and ends this week; back to the *women*, next.

3 October 1962

The piece is being copied out on the typewriter; It looks very different than I thought. I hope to have it all on blue paper by Friday, and rewrite over the weekend.

9 October 1962

My piece is in the 2nd typescript stage, and seems rather imbecilic, at present. V. light in tone. . . . If they don't laugh during the first five minutes, I'll just start cutting, as I go along.

11 October 1962

It is sometimes a good thing—a fortunate development—when a piece of writing turns out to be quite different from what its author originally planned. Change of direction, even after a paper is well started, is, at best, a sign that the facts involved—

and the writer's feeling about the facts—are fairly lively; are not merely a series of clichés or a file of dead notions. They move and breathe, and given their head, often combine and re-combine in interesting and unexpected ways.

—I intended this paper, which I am about to read to you, to be a description (and an analysis) of the work of certain women poets, chiefly American and of this century, as contrasted to women poets of the past and foreshadowing, to a slight degree, women poets of the future. I soon found that this plan would not work, or rather, that it would work only in the most tiresome and boring way. For to tell the truth, there is very little that one can say about women poets, past, present, and (presumably) to come. One truth about them is an open secret: when they are bad they are very very bad, and when they are good they are magnificent. I shall try to say this little as I go along, and I plan to issue a few warnings at the end of these remarks. But the bulk of my talk will be concerned with the achievement of certain remarkable women writers who were not poets, but novelists, critics, and (dreadful word) feminists.

The word feminism today conjures up rather unhappy and dowdy figures; the suffragette stands in most young people's minds, I find, as a sort of large, formidable, virtuous virago. But it is a word which has its own honor and radiance; it was lived for, and sometimes died for, by members of several generations of disenfranchised individuals who, far from representing a persecuted minority, stood for one half of the human race. At present, any woman, in the Western world, who wishes to vote, can; although we tend to forget that French women won that right quite recently, in the Liberation under de Gaulle. The majority of Swiss women do not want to vote, for mountain-bred reasons of their own.

The rights of women as citizens, the facts concerning women as creative human beings, are subjects which have accumulated, and continue to accumulate, an extraordinary array of attack and defense—of panegyric and contumely—much of it of unexampled foolishness. At the moment, we are being told by writers in special numbers of periodicals devoted to the situation of the modern American woman that a new sort of "crypto-feminism" is upon us, and this may well be true; women at present seem to be fighting a battle against automation, on the one hand, and mixed feelings concerning their freedom and leisure, husbands, lovers, and children on the other. The problem of the woman artist remains unchanged. Henry James, in *The Tragic Muse,* spoke of "that oddest of animals, the artist who happens to be born a woman." Robert Graves has more recently said that women poets have a distinctly difficult problem, since they must be their own Muse. Farther back in time, in ancient manuscripts, in inscriptions chiseled into rock and marble, in ideograms, in hieroglyphics, and, of course, in print, the discussion has gone on: woman's nature, her place in society, her charm and her wiles, her physiological and economic dilemmas, her open and her hidden powers—attracting, from men and women alike (but chiefly from men), overweening praise as well as blame; temper, contempt; false and true witness; and spite. These discussions have reached points of particular sharpness and bitterness whenever mankind as a whole has gone over into a crucially new era—when, for example, the male, at the beginning of the age of bronze and the age of iron, began to swagger about his prowess in war, agriculture, and the hunt; when St. Paul began to preach and send pastoral letters to his congregations, around and about the Mediterranean; and at the beginning of the Industrial Revolution, in England and in France.

A full record of the results of these shifts, insofar as they bore on the position of women, appears in meticulously organized detail in Simone de Beauvoir's *Le Seconde Sexe* (Paris, 1949) which I have read in translation. (One frightening moment in my preliminary reading occurred, I might add, when I thought that I was trapped for good in Mlle. de Beauvoir's pages—and I shall return to these.) Of recent years a strong interest, archaeological, poetic, and psychoanalytic, has been focused upon women in pre-history—upon the realm of the Great Mother, upon the rule of the White Goddess—upon the megaliths, the round walls, and the circular tombs of mankind at the matriarchal stage. Here, in this silent kingdom of stones, women are invisible except for a few grotesque figurines, but women in historic antiquity are both visible (in sculpture, on vases, on coins) and vocal (in literature and myth).

At first their manifestation is double: they cherish and they terrify. Cybele, mother of all the gods, with her crown of towers, brought over by the Greeks from the Asian continent, and to be treasured by the Romans; Isis, in the dark backward of Egyptian time, corn goddess, mother of earth and of heaven, sister and wife to Osiris; the Hindu Kali, wife of Siva, goddess, according to one definition, of "feminine energy," with her necklace of skulls. And it was a woman who, at Delphi, the center of the Greek world, uttered the words of the god. It was a woman (Socrates'—or was it Plato's?) Diotima, who, in the manner of all good female teachers down the ages, told the philosopher to follow his daemon; it was a female goddess who gave Athens its name. And, in the opinion of a modern Cambridge Hellenist, it was Spartan women who led the fullest, happiest, best adjusted lives of any women in history. This opinion is rather a blow to the female artist, since Spartan women produced no art of any kind; Sappho was an Eastern Greek from an island off Asia Minor.

Since the beginning of this year, with this paper in mind, I began to gather together a series of quotations wherein opinions for or against the female nature in general or feminine artistic powers in particular, were expressed; and I want to read you a selection of these directly, without paraphrase. The true woman haters are not represented, since their manias —Strindberg's, for example—are all too evident; and the fanatical champions of women show up rarely, but some of these last will be examined. The more kindly disposed satirists make, of course, if one is on woman's side, the pleasantest reading.

"Women are nicer than men," said Lord Byron. Byron made another and far more famous summation of the (to his mind) essential difference of emotional attitude (at least) between the sexes, but since that dictum has become a cliché, and I am trying to avoid clichés, I shall not repeat it here. (Women readers, by the way, hated *Don Juan* when it was first published.) Shaw, who is on the side of women, but critically so (except in the case of St. Joan), in his preface to *Man and Superman* compares women's relentless energy to that of a boa constrictor, and in another passage, having first pointed out that in Shakespeare's plays the woman always takes the initiative, he goes to the insect world for an example to embellish his argument. "The pretense that woman does not take the initiative is part of the farce. Why, the whole world is strewn with the snares, traps, gins and pitfalls for the capture of men by women. Men, on the other hand, attach penalties to marriage, etc. . . . All in vain. Women must marry because the race must perish without her travail. . . . It is assumed that woman must wait, motionless, until she is wooed. Nay, she often does wait motionless. That is the way the spider waits for a fly."

And here is a short passage from a British review of Lewis Mumford's endlessly provocative *The City in History*: "The theme of the whole work is the innate dualism of the human race, forever oscillating between the still and silent female principle, life-conserving, loving, anti-rational, and the restless, argumentative male principle, with its addiction to geometry, mass-organization and war." And, to turn to the Mumford book itself, we find, in the author's discussion of neolithic culture, a description of women's place therein. "Neolithic man's concentration on organic life and growth [involved] not merely a sampling and testing of what nature had provided but a discriminating selection and propagation. . . . Domestication means large changes, first, permanence and continuity in residence, and second, the exercise of control and foresight over processes once subject to the caprices of nature. With this go habits of gentling and nurturing and breeding. Here woman's needs, woman's solicitudes, woman's capacity for gentleness and love, must have played a dominating part. . . . Certainly home and mother are written over every phase of neolithic agriculture. . . . It was woman who wielded the digging stick or the hoe: she who tended the garden crops and accomplished those masterpieces of selection and cross-fertilization which turned raw wild species into the prolific and richly nutritious domestic varieties: who made the first containers, weaving baskets and coiling the first clay

pots. . . . Woman's presence made itself felt in every part
of the village: not least in its physical structures, with their
protective enclosures, whose further symbolic meanings psy-
choanalysis has now tardily brought to light. *Security, recep-
tivity, enclosure, nurture*—these functions belong to woman;
and they take structural expression in the house and the oven,
the byre and the bin, the cistern, the storage pit, the granary
and . . . to pass on to the city, in the wall and the moat, and
all inner spaces, from the atrium to the cloister. House and village, and eventually the town itself, are woman writ large. In
Egyptian hieroglyphics 'house' and 'town' may stand as symbols for 'mother,' as if to confirm the similarity of the individual
and collective nurturing function."

Robert Graves, in *his* endlessly provocative, but more fanciful and illogical treatise, *The White Goddess,* describes at
length the changes which took place at the shift from matriarchy to patriarchy—a shift based, it is now, I believe,
generally agreed, by archaeologists and cultural historians
alike, on man's growing power over metals; on man's discovery of the processes of smelting, first of bronze and then of
iron. The plough superseded the digging tool, and woman's
gentle and wily powers went down before the "sheer dy-
namism" of man's. Many of the consequences were bitter
ones, from the woman's point of view. We hear the full
denunciatory male voice sounding in passage after passage of
the Old Testament; and we come upon the ancient Chinese
concepts of Yin and Yang: Yin, "the female, negative, dark,
evil principle as contrasted to Yang, the male, positive, bright,
beneficent principle"—terms, Webster tells us, "in a dualism
which runs through much of Chinese philosophy, folk-lore,
divination, religion, medicine, science and magic." Here we

seem to come upon not only the harsh terms of a patriarchy, but of a matriarchy reversed, denied, and denigrated.

We do not hear the direct words of women during these harsher periods of masculine power, but we begin to hear their indirect words, long before they were written down. We begin to hear them in Homer—in the words Nausicaa speaks to Ulysses on the seashore and, later, by a pillar of a room in her father's house—dignified and unfrightened; in the words of women sitting by the hearths of their houses, distaff in hand; in the words of Calypso, of Penelope, of Circe (these last two weave, instead of spin). Man's artisanship has now reached the virtuoso stage; what a masterpiece of the smith's art is the shield of Achilles! Man the planner, woman the improviser; a balance has been struck; it is woman's wisdom, as well as man's, that sounds through the Homeric scenes. We are told facts we feel to be true concerning these people; and we recognize female speech, in the mouths of young girls, wives, and sorceresses. A few centuries will pass before we hear a woman uttering, in matchless form, her own words: Sappho's words, as clear and as straightforward and as moving today as when first spoken.

The central tenets of extreme feminism since the Industrial Revolution have been based on the claim that absolute male domination has existed, in an unbroken line, since the dawn of time. These tenets are only partially true. That periods of masculine harshness and intolerance came into being in eras of crucial change is undeniable; that the beginning of the Christian era brought humiliation to womankind we have the words of St. Paul and of the early Church fathers to prove. But at the end of the Middle Ages woman had re-gained her place as a goddess: according to chivalry, "an ideal, a higher being." Beatrice, this being's apotheosis, through her poet, defines and describes Paradise. And as a reform of Christian life and faith began within the Church, in the late thirteenth and early fourteenth centuries, women began to assert themselves in the reforming religious movement. "Awakened to religion, women who only a short time before had been declared by eminent religious teachers to be without souls, began to record their visions and trances and their mysterious experiences in contact with God, in letters, di-aries, and memoirs; and in this way there grew up a wholly distinctive literature of ecstatic confession and self-revelation." These works prefigured the supreme mysticism of the great Teresa, the saint of Avila.

I have just quoted the cultural historian Egon Friedell, who goes on to say: "Here we are in the presence of a fact we shall frequently meet again: that great spiritual movements and emotional revivals very often originate among women. A woman possesses a natural flair for everything that may germinate, every kind of secret growth, everything . . . which is of the future rather than of the present. . . . [Man] is a born professional and expert, but woman is a multiplicity of things. . . ."

The British feminists of the late nineteenth and the early part of the twentieth centuries were fighting free of one of the most restrictive periods in recorded history, so far as the status of women was concerned: the age of Victoria. The strictures of that age had made them harsh and bitter; and we will find Virginia Woolf accusing fathers and sons of depriv-ing daughters and sisters of educations, and of other acts of masculine pride, arrogance, and braggadocio. It is heartening to remember, however, that a young woman who died two years before Victoria was born had already invented the kind of English novel wherein sense and sensibility are, and can be, combined. Jane Austen, who thought of herself as a painter of miniatures, had already placed a cornerstone of prose narrative firmly in its place, in the full light of day, before the (for women) Victorian darkness set in.

The beginning and middle years of Victoria's reign were certainly marked by grotesque excesses of male control, social, political, and familial. We now have, in recorded statistics, the number of benighted governesses (21,000 in 1851), and of ill-paid and sweated seamstresses (70,518 over twenty, and 18,561 under twenty, according to the 1841 census) who then struggled for some sort of livelihood. We also have the number—in six figures—of the domestic servants who, in 1841, waited on the Victorian wives, whose husbands had, quite generally, forced them into enervating idleness. Idleness had become, for women, a class badge; if you were the wife of a prosperous man you did nothing, thereby providing a visible sign of your husband's standing and success. (The middle class was beginning to copy the manners and customs of the aristocracy.) "A girl" (and I'm quoting a sound recent authority) "was trained for the marriage market like a racehorse. Her education consisted of showy accomplishments designed to ensnare young men. The three R's of this deadly equipment were music, drawing and French. Particularly music. It was an article of faith with mother and daughter alike that music was an infallible method of attracting a husband. Once the Victorian girl was seated at the piano with an enraptured swain bending over her, the battle was won. . . . And needlework was considered a most lady-like accomplishment." One writer on the period ties in the Oxford Movement with a rivival of interest in church needlework. "Curates, particularly, stood to profit by gifts of flowers, grapes, jelly—and altarcloths."

The demand of the Victorian male for innocence—and ignorance—left the Victorian woman untrained in the practical conduct of life. The "bustling Chaucerian housewife," the Renaissance manageress of great estates, had largely disappeared. Girls and women now, except in the rarest instances, took on the servile, flattering manners of the slave. Women, often forced by circumstances to resort to an insidious sort of hidden rule, became past mistresses of the cosseting gesture and the seductive wile. Their clothes—the very nearly unmanageable hoopskirt—the tight corseting—made them into puppets. And they were almost helpless under the law, and trapped for good in marriage. But soon they began to break out into open (or half-concealed) rebellion. Florence Nightingale opened the way: "Her departure for the Crimea lit a torch which was never to be put out. Slowly and surely the status of nursing was raised, and this led women to clamor for [other] professional and business opportunities."

A very nearly complete documentation of the life and surroundings of the nineteenth century English woman has come down to us, through novels written by women's pens. From the mills of the Midlands to the parlors of the high bourgeoisie; from the Yorkshire moors to the great house, we have it all—written down by women who are training their ears by instinct, and are learning to cast brave and penetrating glances into the hearts and souls of their characters.

Early in the twentieth century, the power of women writers to introduce radical innovations into form comes clearly into view. In my reading I was happy to rediscover Dorothy Richardson. Dorothy Richardson, born in 1882, died in obscurity in 1957. The last book of her series of novels (which bears the all-over title of *Pilgrimage*) was published in the early 1930s; and the series, I was delighted to find, is still in print. Richardson was a crucially important transitional figure, being certainly one of the first, if not the first, writer to introduce the stream-of-consciousness technique into English fiction. It is a matter of literary record that Joyce's *A Portrait of the Artist as a Young Man* first appeared in *The Egoist*, a periodical published in London, from February 1914 through September 1915. Dorothy Richardson, according to her own statement, quoted by her publishers, began to write *Pointed Roofs*, the first volume of the *Pilgrimage* sequence, in 1913. *Pointed Roofs* was published in 1915; *A Portrait* appeared in book form the following year.

In 1915 poetry in English had recently experienced the impact of the Imagist group (which included one woman and several Americans). What is called Impressionism struck the novel late; the results were to be astonishing.

Dorothy Richardson's description of the youth and young womanhood of a middle-class English girl, working as a governess and as a clerk, first in Germany and in the English countryside, and then in London, at the turn of the century, is remarkable enough to be considered on its own terms, quite apart from Joyce's chronicle of his own boyhood and youth, in Dublin. In Richardson, from the beginning, and perhaps most purely in the mid-stream of the narrative, we come upon technical innovation always closely allied to the matter in hand—never artificially superimposed—together with a delicacy of perception which sometimes amounts to a kind of clairvoyance. This originality is bound up, it is true, with a certain naïveté of mind and with what often seems to be a deliberate awkwardness of expression. "She works with memory," one critic has said of her, "[and] what must amaze most people is the apparently wilful choice of unpicturesque, unpromising, unideal, and in many instances actually unpleasant aspects of reality. Yet all these queer things . . . are treated by her with their ramifications and convolutions as if they were carefully selected ideal symbols of human life." And Richardson will go over and over an idea with stubborn insistence; her language sometimes stammers in her effort to project her perceptions and her convictions with adequate force. She possesses "a certain obstinate, humorous, massive, deliberate approach to life which is not in the least degree ashamed of being pedantic."

Her attitude, in what, over the years, turned out to be a series of autobiographical narratives, is feminist in a very special and unorthodox way. She is not at all obsessed by any fixed notion that men have been continuously out to conquer, subdue, and enslave women, and she has sharp words for female ruses. In deploring women's flattery of the male she attacks a feminine defense-mechanism, cultivated to a fantastic extent in mid-Victorian society. Woman, she says, should claim her birthright as a being whose knowledge of, and intuition concerning, reality are profound. Richardson's attitude toward the masculine nature and male assumptions in general ranges between pity and irritation. She lived through the pre-1914 suffrage agitation without being in any way involved with its physical violence. For Richardson, the difference between the nature of man and the nature of woman was "abysmal." Politics and the vote touched the surface only.

"These woman's rights people," she says with characteristic forthrightness in *Deadlock*, the sixth of her volumes, published in 1921, "are the worst of all. Because they think women have been 'subject' in the past. Women have never been subject. Never can be. The proof of this is the way men have always been puzzled and everlastingly trying fresh theories; founded on the very small experience of women any man is capable of having. Disabilities, imposed by law, are a stupid insult to women, but have never touched them as individuals. In the long run they injure only men. For they have kept back the civilization of the outside world, which is the only thing men can make. It is not everything. It is a sort of result, poor and shaky, because the real inside civilization of women, the one thing that has been in them from the first, and is not in the natural man—not made by things—is kept out of it. Women do not need civilization. It is apt to bore them. They keep it back. That does not matter, to themselves. But it matters to men. And if they want their old civilization to be anything but a dreary-weary puzzle, they must leave off imagining themselves as a race of gods fighting against chaos, and thinking of women as part of the chaos they have to civilize. There isn't any 'chaos.' . . . It's the principal masculine delusion. It is not a truth to say that women must be civilized."

Well, there you have her—in part: the brave little wrong-headed-to-the-majority partisan of her own sex, in her high-necked blouse and long skirt, from which the dust and mud of the London streets must be brushed daily; working long hours in poor light at a job which involves physical drudgery as well as endless tact (she was a fashionable dentist's assistant); going home to a tiny bedroom under the roof of a badly run boardinghouse; meeting, in spite of her handicapped position, an astonishing range of kinds of human beings; going to lectures; listening to debates at the Fabian Society (of which she became a member); daring to go into a restaurant late at night, driven by cold and exhaustion, to order a roll, butter, and a cup of cocoa; trying to write, truthfully and as a woman; loving her friends, her country week-ends, her London. And continually sensing transition; welcoming change; eager to bring on the future. And reiterating: "Until it had been clearly explained that men were always partly wrong in their ideas, life would be full of poison and secret bitterness."

And here is an excerpt from one of her passages of pure "mystic" joy. "For a moment [Miriam] found herself back in her own sense of existence, gazing at the miraculous spectacle of people and things, existing; herself, however, perplexed and resourceless, within it, everything sinking into insignificance beside the fact of being alive, having lived on to another moment of unexplainable glorious happiness."

Innocence. Impatience. Improvisational awkwardness, if you will. But without any doubt we find in this (then) young woman a woman's perceptions, in full upward flight, a woman's sense of the worth of her womanhood, richly displayed. "Her work," said Wilson Follett, in a preface to *Deadlock*, "was the first definitive expression in the English novel of the whole, self-tortured modern consciousness, together with the precise idiom in which it does its thinking. . . . She masters her subject not by analyzing it from a strategic angle, but by achieving complete identity with it throughout. [This method, this contemporary development] is so completely crystallized in the work of Miss Richardson, its pioneer, that it would stand thereafter as a *fait accompli*, by virtue of her work alone."

Virginia Woolf (1882–1941), daughter of Sir Leslie Stephen, eminent man of letters, by his second wife, was not an innovator, in any true sense. She had the faculty, however, of responding to, and absorbing, certain floating and pervasive notions in the literary atmosphere of her time, in a way that combined brilliance with subtlety. She resuscitated the moribund "casual" literary essay, bringing to it "the play of an extraordinary intuition and taste for values." The first volume of *The Common Reader,* wherein her essays were first collected, appeared in 1925, and a second volume, in 1932, helped to shift the angle of the period's critical approach away from the stiffly factual and didactic toward edged wit and serene balanced insight. She had definite limitations—she could not, for example, summon the detachment with which she treated figures of the past when discussing her contemporaries: *Ulysses* was a catastrophe and D. H. Lawrence a vulgarian. She had had the good fortune to be born a member of a literate and articulate circle, and at its best her writing has all the life and vividness of good talk. And her warmth and generosity, happily, are strikingly evident in her portrayal of the talent of English women writers of the eighteenth and nineteenth centuries. How good she is on the subject of Elizabeth Barrett, later Elizabeth Barrett Browning, for example. "Her mind was lively and secular and satirical," she says, and she gives this Victorian woman full credit for harboring the unlikely ambition of dealing with the life of her time in verse. This ambition was misdirected, but, Virginia Woolf goes on to say, "*Aurora Leigh* remains, for all its imperfections, a book that still lives and breathes and has its being."

And how perceptive she is on the Brontës. She names Charlotte a poet as well as Emily: "*Wuthering Heights* was a greater book than *Jane Eyre* because Emily was a greater poet than Charlotte. There is no *I* in *Wuthering Heights.*

There are no governesses. There are no employers. There is love, but not the love of men and women. Emily was inspired by some more general conception. . . . Hers [was] the rarest of all powers. She could free life from its dependence on facts: . . . indicate the spirit of a face so that it needs no body: by speaking of the moor make the wind blow and the thunder roar." And no clearer or more definite praise has ever been given by one woman writer to another than the praise given in Virginia Woolf's long and penetrating essay on Jane Austen to "the most perfect artist among women, the writer whose works are immortal."

Virginia Woolf's own command over the novel was subject to lapses in plan and in power; *To the Lighthouse* (1927) and *Between the Acts* (1941), however, prove her dramatic sense of time and change and of the tragic diversity of human character and loyalties. In these two novels her feminism is in abeyance—a feminism based, as I have said, on the classic (in her youth) concept of woman materially enslaved and creatively baffled by the unbreakable historic dominance of man. In *A Room of One's Own* (1929), based on lectures given at Newnham and Girton, she stated her case with the most charming scholarship and wit; in *Three Guineas* (1938) the insistence on masculine dominance has become obsessive, and the protesting voice shrill. The male—at least the British male—is now seen actually to conspire against the female. Male regalia—those legal wigs, for example—those academic gowns and mortarboards—those religious mitres and copes—were invented, not as the distinguishing signs of a profession (and class) but of a bullying sex. And in the case of military uniforms—here again the British male had the subjugation of sister, mother, sweetheart, daughter, wife, aunt, and female cousins to a distant degree, in mind. Those horsehair plumes, helmets, visors, shining cuirasses, epaulets; that quantity of gold braid; those gloves and hip boots and bright buttons and colored stripes and bindings—even, one might say, by a slight extension of the indictment, all those pistols, swords and medals—had become to Mrs. Woolf symbols of masculine pride, invented, over the centuries, to keep women in their place.

This kind of feminism, which leaps all barriers of common sense, is not found, except in small and rather backward enclaves, in England or America today. But the fact that it continues to exist in France in a somewhat altered form, the work of Mlle. Simone de Beauvoir proves. At moments, as one reads the more argumentative works of this remarkable woman, the atmosphere seems to shift into the region of the fairy-tale, particularly of that fairy-tale in which a girl, working under an enchanter's spell, spins a roomful of straw into gold. In the case of Mlle. de Beauvoir, the task has been reversed: the gold of life is over and over again transformed into the straw of "existential ethics" (her phrase).

Ostensibly, of course, reason rules. With patient scholarly minuteness Mlle. de Beauvoir sets before us, in perfectly organized passages, her feminist argument, backed up by data based on recorded myth as well as historic fact and on the findings of the sciences. She seems to play her cards with the utmost fairness (given her anti-masculine bias); her evidence bristles with testifiable truths and clear-headed conclusions. But as she proceeds into the second section of her tireless work, *The Second Sex*, a faint suspicion arises in the mind of the reader that, even if women were free, Beauvoir considers them unable to conduct their lives with true wisdom and fortitude, or to enter into a true "brotherhood" with men. Her attitude becomes openly ambivalent, somewhere on, or around, her five hundred and sixtieth page. Women chatter; women are forever trying to converse, to adapt, to arrange, rather than to destroy and build anew; they prefer compromise and adjustment to revolution. . . . But "let the future be opened to them and they [may] no longer desperately cling to the past. . . . Today . . . woman's situation inclines her to seek salvation in literature and art. Living marginally to the masculine world, she sees it not in its universal form, but from her special point of view. For her it is no conglomeration of implements and concepts, but a source of sensations and emotions. . . . Taking an attitude of negation or denial, she is not absorbed in the real: she protests against it with words. . . . To prevent an inner life that has no useful purpose from sinking into nothingness . . . she must resort to self-expression. Then, too, it is well known that she is a chatterer and a scribbler. With a little ambition she will be found writing her memoirs, making her biography into a novel, breathing forth her feelings in poems. The vast leisure she enjoys is most favorable to such activities!" (Exclamation point mine.)

In this manner the later pages of *The Second Sex* turn rapidly from the comparatively cool and detached exposition, which characterized earlier sections, into a series of bitter diatribes against the modern "creative" woman—particularly the woman writer. This writer cheats; she creates mirages; "she will not be capable of sustained and persistent effort; she will never succeed in gaining a solid technique. . . . The majority of women would-be writers, at the moment when [they] think of themselves as most original . . . actually [do] no more than reinvent a banal cliché."

And, in a final burst of what has turned into an almost unbroken tone of petulance, she says: "Not that these independent women lack originality in behavior or feelings; on the contrary, some are so singular that they should be locked up; all in all, many of them are more whimsical, more eccentric, than the men whose discipline they reject. . . . There are women who are mad and there are women of sound method; none has that madness in her that we call genius."

Nor, we are bound to conclude, will they ever have, even when, in a "supreme victory . . . by and through their natural differentiation, men and women [will] unequivocally affirm their *brotherhood*." In spite of all her protestations to the contrary, we feel, as we come to the end of this extraordinary work, that Mlle. de Beauvoir cherishes, in the deep recesses of her existentially trained self, a dislike, even a contempt, for the enigmatic, the intuitive, the graceful, the tender, the opalescent, the mercurial side of women's nature— the side that truly complements the virtues of the male. The side that has always been involved centrally in the production of women's art; the side that contributes, as one critic has said, "to the deeply feminine appeal and enchantment of Berthe Morisot's [and Mary Cassatt's] pictures"; the side which the great women poets have drawn upon; the side which sustains the great women novelists. This feeling is reinforced as, just before we close the book, we glance at its formidable index.

I recommend to you, on some afternoon of rain and incipient boredom, the perusal of this index, and the ticking off of the names of women artists listed therein. The gaps and *lacunae* are shocking. Beauvoir has left out very nearly every woman of any striking genius, down the years of recorded history, and those she has included are given short shrift. On the other hand, she has listed numbers of mediocrities, French, American and British (chiefly modern), and a good many nonentities (chiefly French). Colette receives the largest number of mentions, which is all to the good. But where is Louise Labé, the great sonnet writer of Lyons, in the time of the *Pléiade?* Where is Mme. de Sevigné (a line or two); where is Emily Dickinson (a slighting remark)? St. Teresa is given her due: "She lived out, as a woman, an experience whose meaning goes far beyond the fact of her sex. . . . But she is a striking exception. . . . What her minor sisters have given us is an essentially feminine vision of the world and of salvation; it is not transcendence that they seek: it is the redemption of their femininity."

Femininity. We close the book, not without a relieved sigh, and turn to a set of remarks written, in the second volume of his autobiography, by Leonard Woolf, Virginia Woolf's husband. "I have always been greatly attracted," he says, "by the undiluted female mind. And I mean the adjective 'undiluted' for I am not thinking of exceptional minds, like Cleopatra or Mrs. Carlyle or Jane Austen or Virginia Woolf; I am thinking of the 'ordinary' woman, undistinguished, often unintellectual and unintrospective. The minds of most women differ from the minds of most men in a way which I feel very distinctly, but which becomes rather indistinct as I try to describe it. Their minds seem to me to be gentler, more sensitive, more civilized. Even in many stupid, vain, tiresome women this quality is often preserved below the exasperating surface. But it is not easy to catch it or bring it to the surface. You can only do so by listening to, and by being really interested in, what they say. I think I have taught myself gradually to be interested in what women say to me, and to listen attentively to what they are saying, for in this way you get now and again a glimpse, or rather a *breath* of this pure, curiously female quality of mind. It is the result, I suppose, partly of their upbringing which is usually so different from that of the male in all classes, and partly of fundamental, organic differences of sex. And that again, I suppose, is why, as a male, I get a romantic, even perhaps a sentimental, pleasure from feeling the quality."

In women's deportment, we can agree, the brutal, rough, swaggering, masculinized gesture never, somehow, works, the cigars of the young George Sand and the middle-aged Amy Lowell to the contrary notwithstanding. And in her writing, the gentle, tender, nurturing feminine nature perhaps precludes ultimate coarseness and harshness, either in tone or in choice of material. Women have never succeeded, for example, in writing true surrealism*—a style closely involved with the hallucinatory, the shocking, and the terrifying effect; with the calculated irrational and the direct or indirect erotic. A younger generation of women poets have allied themselves with "far-out" poetic procedures; unsuccessfully. For (and I have looked into this subject with some care) these younger women writers, although published side by side, in anthologies and elsewhere, with their far-out brothers, cannot bring themselves to use Anglo-Saxon monosyllables of a sexual or scatological kind. They swear a little, instead. (Even Mary McCarthy, even Caitlin Thomas.) (An exception to this rule has recently appeared in England. In her long and rather chaotic novel *The Golden Notebook,* Doris Lessing, born in Persia and brought up in Southern Rhodesia, permits herself every license of language. I recommend the results to your attention.)

Fortunately, this limitation in vocabulary does not mean

---

* Except, perhaps, in the case of Djuna Barnes, who is more Joycean than surrealist.

that young women writers today are in any way limited in regard to subject matter. In fact, only recently a young woman
of nineteen broke through several taboos formerly prevalent
in the British theatre. This was Shelagh Delaney, whose
play *A Taste of Honey,* after a great success both in London
and New York, has been made into a most poignant motion-
picture. "Down from Salford came this splendid young proph-
etess," Colin MacInnes, in *Encounter,* recently remarked.

Like all prophetesses Shelagh Delaney tells the truth—her
own truth, both observed and suffered through. For in the case
of the woman writer and particularly of the woman poet,
every lie—every fib, even—shows, like a smutch on a child's
(or on a woman's) cheek. We can, perhaps, at this point
draw up a short list of tentative rules. First, in literature (or
in any other art) women must not lie. Second, they must not
whine. Third, they must not attitudinize (in the role of the
femme fatale least of all). And they must neither theatrical-
ize nor coarsen their truths. They must not be vain, and they
must not flight or kite in any witch-like way. Nor, on the
other hand, go in for little girlishness and false naïveté. Nor
"stamp a tiny foot at the universe."

So far as form is concerned, they should consider themselves free to move about unhampered by strict rules, keeping
in mind, however, the fact that women can be, and have
been, superb technicians. Perhaps the long *souffle—the big machine,* as the French say—is not for them; on the other hand
it may lie ahead of them, in the discernible future. One or
two warnings concerning form *can* be issued. A lengthy period
should be allowed to elapse before the sonnet-sequence devoted to the triumph, sorrows, and bafflements of love, be
revived by women writers. I say revived, for at the moment
the form is, fortunately, dead. And as it was women who

helped to bring such sequences to high brilliance, it was women, in number, who were guilty, especially in England, of its nineteenth- and twentieth-century decadence. It is a particularly insidious addiction, this fondness for sonnets in a connected series, and one which, Heaven knows, men invented and have shared. Its dangers for feminine talent are apparent: it allows women to go on and on, either praising the lover or blaming him. It also allows shows of complete and utter subservience (women rarely write sonnets in a mood of rebellion). It allows, in fact, infinite, hair-splitting wrangling. And it all too frequently brings in a rather artificial death-wish—a kind of graveyardism—not at all in the true, simple, and poignant vein of the complaints of those poor miserable girls who, in the anonymous ballads, ask for a stone to be put at their head and feet when they lie under the wild goose grasses. Rather a death-wish that smells of the lamp. . . .

What did the women say? Well, they said many things which closely resemble words said by their brothers, lovers, husbands, fathers, and sons. They have never issued so many peremptory commands, or drawn up so many propositions composed of abstract terms, as have men. But they have asked, as woman and artist, the same questions men have asked: Who am I? From whence did I come? Is there a design in the universe of which I am a part? Do you love me? Shall I die forever?

Women have said: "The moon has set, and the Pleiades; midnight has passed, and still I lie alone." They have said: "I *am* Heathcliff" and "Circumference is my business" and "No coward soul is mine." They have told great stories—Lady Murasaki and Scheherazade—and, in our own day, Karen Blixen (Isak Dinesen). And a kind of ambience of anonymous women's poetry and song floats through every culture: their proverbs, their happy nonsense in *Ma Mère L'Oie* and in *Mother Goose*, their chilling improvisations in ballad and fairy-tale—their tenderness in the rhymes devised to quiet a restless child, or put it to sleep.

The blows dealt women by social and religious change were real, and in certain times and places definitely maiming. But the articulate woman has always made it clear that she recognizes those biological and psychic laws which make her, as a modern eclectic analyst has recently pointed out, not the opposite or the "equal" (or the rival) of man, but man's complement.

Women still have within them the memory of the distaff and the loom—and, we must remember, the memory of the dark, cruel, wanton goddesses. But because woman rarely has gone over, in the past, to a general and sustained low complicity or compliance in relation to her companion, man, we can hope for her future.

And she listens, when a truly sibylline utterance falls from a sister's lips, such as the remark of the late Karen Blixen (surely one of the great writers of our or any other time) when she said: "Men and women are two locked caskets, of which each contains the key to the other." She listens to these words, with their ring of mysterious truth, with awe—not terror.

❦ ❦

Your letter came just after my return from Peterborough, and just before my two rather taxing "jobs" in October: 1) a paper read at Bennington (called "What the Women Said") and 2) an appearance (and a set of notes *and* a reading) at the great Library of Congress Poetry Festival. Both of these do's went off v. well. The audience at Bennington laughed in the right places—and it *was* a *well-written* lecture. The original assignment had been women poets; but I must say this topic came to bore me excessively, as I sat in my studio at MacDowell, drinking coffee and feeding the open fire with massive logs. —So I just wrote about women, in and out of literature—poets *and* novelists, from the Bronze Age (Homer) on!

14 Back through stars

ᴋ ᴋ

8 JANUARY/54

These cold winter days—but the sun has turned. It is in Capricorn, and the light is longer, one minute a day. How wonderful: the winter and summer solstices; the vernal and autumn equinoxes! Now I treasure each slightest move of the seasons: the sun coming back; day and night equal; the days longer than the nights; the equal point reached again; the nights longer than the days. Another—what Jünger calls "the starry"—dimension is added to existence—added late. . . .

12 January/54

The snow. The sound of shovels. The *up*-light and the silence.

Waking in the morning in the winter, in this apartment, the ancient pipes begin to hiss, around 7:00 A.M.; and this wakens me. How calm, how *cozy*, how detached I am, in my single bed, in an actual bed-*room* (for the first time in many years). How I should be fortified: how I *am* fortified. . .

Looking into the journal I kept during the 1933 European journey—I see how, at the time, the power of seeing and hearing and noting down had developed. The diary kept in Vienna in 1922 was without any real descriptive power. Then, I could only describe through a set of symbols—poetically, lyrically. Straight rendering completely baffled me; I remember this. So inner, so baffled, so *battered*—even at 24—that I *noticed* practically nothing; or, if I did notice it, I could not put it down (in prose) with any directness of effect. —So that there is no description of Frau Weinberger, going around the room with her duster and lorgnette; no description of Trudi, with her smooth hair and pretty teeth; no description of the streets, cafés, restaurants . . . the weather . . . the clothes . . . the manners and customs. Of course, I knew almost nothing about contemporary human life. . . . Historically I could see a little . . . but not in a flash. Get at the quotidian essence . . .

Embroidering and listening to music, for an hour or two a day, has given me a break from endless reading and *obligatory* writing. This "long prose thing" will help me, I trust and pray, to get back to pure writing *as such*: to "creative" writing, as the phrase goes. To the capable and free setting down of "memory and desire" . . . of what I have become, and what I know. —It has been so hard for me "to make a full breast." . . . Perhaps by spring, I can square up to the task, instead of writing cross-handed, as it were, and cross-seated, at a table edge. . . .

1 FEBRUARY/54

V. Woolf's *A Writer's Diary*: usually done in "fifteen minutes before dinner." —What a monster of egotism she was! —But how touching that, for many years, she had only 13/ a week to spend—about \$3.25, I suppose, from 1912 on. How I have always disliked *Mrs. Dalloway*, with its attempt to *care* for the poor young man; its hatred of doctors (she had already had a brush with psychiatry, it seems, and could not like it!); its frightful sentimentality. . . . And *Orlando*—that "Sapphic" (to use a word of hers) pastiche . . . She had the advantage (if one can use such a word for a semi-cursed thing) of "mood swings"—"the brain turning," etc. Surely, toward the end, that crowd of great spirits and sensitive minds—her friends—should have seen her mounting depression and protected her against herself.

30 AUGUST/54

The two thrilling ovations to the season's turn: cries wrung out of the equinox:

> *L'automne déjà!* and
>
> *Bientôt nous plongerons dans les froides ténèbres;*
> *Adieu, vive clarté de nos étés trop courts!*
>
> —*C'était hier l'été; voici l'automne!*

But the sound of a day of soaking rain—the wind of a real northeaster whipping against the north windows—how refreshing it is! A whole world comes back: the shut-in, the *working* winter world. At this moment of premature storm, I look forward, and *into,* it with joy. . . .

The ice floats close to the shore of the river. I really love these winter days alone. But I should have somewhere to go, in February, where I can see the whole sweep of the winter heaven, at night. It is not good to be shut away from the stars.

17 JANUARY/58

Long hiatus!

A period in which I have learned a great deal. That, for example, at my present age, one is permitted hope but not *ambition*. Ambition is automatically stopped by the thought of death; it becomes trivial and vulgar. But four years ago, just before the two books were published—after being out of print for so long—a little ambition was right and salutary. Since then there have been too many *ending* and *eternity* dreams—some of which I must put down—the recurring *vestibule* dream in particular.

Young Phelps, who runs his life by the stars! What a pleasure and relief to have a faith or a superstition of any kind! I should think that believers would dance with joy in the streets! Some of Yeats' immense confidence and drive, in his old age, came from his belief that he had *successfully* "tampered with the universe." His early naïve belief in magic practices had faded out, but he had brought his fanciful themes into a coherent whole (in *A Vision*), and some of Blake's certainty had become his own (although he was never a true visionary).

Elizabeth Mayer: at 75 she never for a moment either thinks she is old, or projects her age in mood or word. She is gradually thinning down, fading out, in her body; she shows no sign whatever of aging, in her mind or emotions. The books lie on the table; the piano is open and has music on it; she is going to the library tomorrow. . . . And the room flowers around her: the coffee on the table; the square silver box of sugar; the plants in the window. The daughter of Lutheran pastors, she somehow has faith in her bones. . . .

It interests me exceedingly to know where Uranus and Jupiter, for the moment, stand in my horoscope. And I shall go with Herman S. to the Am. Soc. for Psych. R. Why not? The mystery draws in. One needs the help of the imagination to die. . . .

8 JUNE/59

(The landlocked vista: at its end that view which most nearly corresponds to peace in the heart: the horizon.)

୧ ୧

10 JUNE/59

Deep blue hydrangeas bloomed by the houses, in autumn.

Sometimes, at night, one window would be lit, far away.

There were sounds of iron-rimmed wheels, of horses' hooves, of train whistles, of roosters, of voices only a field away, of water going over the mill dam. At the railway crossings stood crossed boards painted in black and white letters, and the diagonally black and white striped wooden barriers came down, before the train went through. The signalman's hut, beside the crossing, was furnished with lanterns, a lunch-box, and a dirty red flag.

17 JUNE/59

The horse stood between the shafts with his head lowered and his ears twitching in the wind. The bank in front of the house was matted over, in places, with last year's oak leaves. The furniture in the wagon looked ugly and forlorn in the cloudy daylight: the up-ended chairs stuck their legs up from a bundle of quilts and heavy draperies; behind them, the rough thicket that ran along the edge of the road; leaves and stems and branches were shaken in the wind. The doors to the house were propped open by bits of rock from the road.

The house was clapboarded, with a slate mansard roof; it stood high on a bank with an oak tree before it and a veranda ran around it on two sides. A flight of wooden steps ran up the bank to the foot of the veranda. Under the mansard eaves, two bands of fancy clapboarding—a row of zigzags and a row of scallops—added to the elegance of the slate roof. Inside, the smell of plaster and dusty floors blew along with every draft, and the worn green window shades flapped loudly at the top of the open sash windows. The windows looked out on the thickets, over the well in the yard, and toward houses two fields away.

This was Oak Street, the first house we lived in, in Ballard-vale. At first, everything went surprisingly well in it.

20 JUNE/59

Something which she thought ridiculous and unfinished in her face—as though part of her had stopped living or had not lived enough; and now, when resistance in the nerves or in the mind, or hope in the heart, was growing less, these unfinished things came out, in her face.

Casting back, what we get is (often) the faces of fools and madmen; wooden railings of old hotels in towns whose distance from one another is measured by the speed of horses' feet; bandstands standing under shrivelling trees and vows made too early or too late. . . .

Sunday afternoon, the suburbs (circa 1912): Two girls, or a group of young men, walk through the streets of wooden houses, under the leaden sky of fall. A great emptiness and desolation, as of everything covered, ended, and withdrawn. Nothing to do, nowhere to go. Away from the flats in the wooden houses after Sunday dinner—from dishwashing and bickering—the young go out in groups of three and four, or two by two, and saunter in the chill wind.

The yellow cinquefoil; the delicate "innocent," half blue, like skim milk, with a thread-like stem; the hepatica in the woods, touched with purple at the heart; the false Solomon's seal on woody banks, and jack-in-the-pulpits growing in hundreds along the watercourses in the pastures . . .

The thing to thank God for (I said, looking down at the counter heaped with small, vivid objects) is the presence of the sunlight and the absence of mental anguish (in which I lived, like a fish in jelly, for so long). It was a heavy pain within the heart; like a voice, it prompted incidence and evil, within the ear. It was like a dreadful fire lit by chance —an undermining fire bred by pressure—self-fed, self-engendered. . . .

How I used to pity the hopeful little men and women who opened stores and sat waiting for someone to come in to buy!

(Within the rooms of houses, seen as a child from the outside) I thought that something must be going on: that people must be achieving something to assail the dreadful monotony of day after day. I trusted them to be doing something. Whatever it was, was as yet closed to me, but these fronts of buildings, with afternoon light falling upon them with such terrible, dramatic effect—these certainly were important. Within them, life burned, a life in which I as yet had no part. I believed this; from my soul I believed it. . . .

SATURDAY 17 SEPTEMBER/60
We must not bring back and describe "the bad mother"—"the Dragon mother"—in order to justify ourselves. Only to understand. —To hold the portrait of this evil figure unresolved, into age, is madness. It should be resolved in late youth. (The last Chinese box . . .) The artist must resolve it into art . . . the man of action into action . . . the philosopher into ideas. After a certain age one should glimpse it most often as a dream—or v. infrequently in *consciously* evoked meaning. . . .

. . . the great kindling power of passionate love, which in age we either do not have or do not allow ourselves to feel . . . with women the inhibition is particularly strong: there are so many ways in which they can make fools of themselves. . . .

SUNDAY 18 SEPTEMBER/60
The Buried Day—C. Day Lewis, p. 122: ". . . like most

budding artists, I had a great capacity for laziness . . . I needed, without knowing why, those times of apparent inaction, apathy almost, when the mind is passive like a net swayed by deep-sea currents, taking in whatever comes its way."

Thursday 7 September/61

The Fitzwilliam incident. It could be expanded and deepened: after the picnic on the beach, the journey with the unexpected companions could lead into a continued series of the unexpected: into death. —The meticulous house of Miss Seal. No blotter on the old desk—but piles of little notebooks . . . The drawing over the desk, the work of Mr. Metcalf, who had just returned from Italy. The charming bathroom, with a pale-green cake of Castile soap, and old pharmacy bottles. The plants: the big begonia with polished leaves and the tiny ivy. The garden: phlox against tall asparagus ferns . . . Scabiosa and nicotiana, in varied colors . . . A fantastic field of chance . . .

The body becomes undependable . . . the mind becomes detached . . . the affections do not disappear, but change into different things (impulses). The *center* of the philosopher's stone . . .

❧ ❧

The fine pleating under the mushroom cap; the cut design of maple and fern. Chance? No . . .

The mushrooms: brown-violet, white and cream. One wishes to make a bouquet of them.

The mystery of the *ordinariness*.

I can't believe in the divinity of Christ, so I'm not a Christian. But of course I believe in the Mystery. (We exist, the fruit of powers beyond us, within us, which we must in some manner trust.) All this order cannot be accident or coincidence. Think of the eye developing in the darkness of the womb!

For some people, though, the Church is perfect. And imagine how pleasant to believe you were going to heaven. Why should it be dull? God has infinite variety; he'd surely think of things for us to do.

In the convent—that one year as a child I spent in the convent—we had to get up at six and go into the church without breakfast. I used to faint regularly . . . just keel over. Very comfortable feeling. Then I was excused and used to be given water biscuits and peanut butter. The convent civilized me: I used to go up into the attic and throw things; they broke me of all that.

MONDAY 18 SEPTEMBER/61
Reflections on a Marine Venus—L. Durrell, p. 48: "Writing poetry educates one into the nature of the game—which is humanity's profoundest activity. In their star-dances the savages try to unite their lives to those of the heavenly bodies—to mix their quotidian rhythms into those great currents which keep the wheels of the universe turning. Poetry attempts to provide much the same sort of link between the muddled inner man with his temporal preoccupations and the uniform flow of the universe outside. Of course everyone is conscious of these impulses; but poets are the only people who do not drive them off.

"Poems, like water-colours, should be left to dry properly

before you alter them—six months or six hours according to the paints you use."

The wild, bold talents as opposed to the merely overdone. . . . Later poetry should be crisp and mad. . . .

C. Parker saying at breakfast: "But 66 is *young, young!*" (She is 75.)

The sad attraction of the sensed impossible situation . . . *Sad*, but neither melancholy nor tragic . . .

TUESDAY 19 SEPTEMBER/61

I have written a poem about a cat. Now I must write one about a dragonfly.

A yellow butterfly crossed my path. "Good luck!" I said to myself.

THE DRAGONFLY

You are made of almost nothing
But of enough
To be great eyes
And diaphanous double vans;
To be ceaseless movement,
Unending hunger
Grappling love.

Link between water and air,
Earth repels you.
Light touches you only to shift into iridescence
Upon your body and wings.

Twice-born, predator,
You split into the heat.
Swift beyond calculation or capture
You dart into the shadow
Which consumes you.

You rocket into the day.
But at last, when the wind flattens the grasses,
For you, the design and purpose stop.

And you fall
With the other husks of summer.

(It is all based on FACT. And I am rather proud of the last line
—which is a piece of pure "inspiration." Get those repeated *u*
sounds—one of them disguised.)

20 SEPTEMBER/61

Wisdom of the years: "I will not make it difficult for others.
Neither will I make it difficult for myself."

Good free-verse *rejects*. I could not use "dark-blue" or
"netted" in the dragonfly poem.

21 SEPTEMBER/61

Terrible dreams! —A morning of lovely wind and rain. The
tail-end of the hurricane. Why do these storms now come so
far north? In the nineteenth century they kept to the southern
tip of the continent. . . . The earth has shifted infinitesi-
mally on its axis. . . .

"The wind will start around noon." A triumph of our age: it can foretell the wind. . . .

The desire (and need) remains to write of a time which has disappeared, and cannot be seen again, except in memory; which in essence or in fact the young cannot experience. A few old stories . . . But not egoistic or *minor* ones . . .

"And all things are forgiven, and it would be strange not to forgive"—this Chekhov knew. Forgiveness and the eagerness *to protect*: These keep me from putting down the crudest shocks received from seven on. With my mother, my earliest instinct was to protect—to take care of, to endure. This, Dr. Wall once told me, is the instinct of a little boy. . . . Well, there it is. I *did* manage to become a woman. . . . Now, in my later years, I have no hatred or resentment left. But I still cannot describe some of the nightmares lived through, with love. So I shan't try to describe them at all. Finished. Over. The door is open, and I see the ringed hand on the pillow; I weep by the hotel window as she goes down the street, with *another*; I stare at the dots which make up the newspaper photograph (which makes me realize that I then had not yet learned to read). The chambermaid tells me to stop crying. How do we survive such things? But it is long over. And forgiven . . .

It is too late either to pour it out or to reconstruct it, bit by bit. What mattered got into the poems. Except for one or two *stories*, which I may be able to tell, it is all there. With the self-pity left out.

And the poems depended on the *ability* to love. (Yeats kept saying this, to the end.) The *faculty* of loving. A talent.

A gift. "We must always be a little in love," Elizabeth M. said to me (at 70!). . . . Yes, but it becomes a difficult *task*. And one that must be dissembled.

≥ ≥

The regions and countries of the dream. The unconscious makes its repeated mistakes; it has not *seen* the reality; it has sensed it merely. The dream Venice is not the Venice experienced; it is all a little wrong. A separate and distinct country is built up, from childhood on, in the dream.

To trace the dream-landscape that has grown inside me every night, all my life, along with daylight reality, and which has mountains, ruins, islands, shores, cities, and even *suburbs* and summer "resorts" *of its own*, related to one another and, many times, recurrent (almost in the sense of revisited).

It has its gardens, its hills, and its sea. Other than ours. A reflection; a distortion . . . And it repeats its mistakes, as though it had learned them by rote. . . .

A perfectly finished and detailed dream in which one says, "But this *is* real: look at the reality of those satin curtains: the light reflects on them so perfectly that there can be no doubt of their reality." And, as a further proof, there is a small collection of medals laid out on a piece of red velvet on the corner of a chest of drawers. "That's the sort of thing that one never *dreams*!"

≥ ≥

Surrealism bores me.

My gift depended on the flash—on the *aperçu*. The fake

reason, the surface detail, language only—these give no joy.

Jiménez kept on with the little flashes to the end. One can only remain open, and wait. . . .

(Earlier)

How can we explain the places where we finally land, after inexplicable journeys, long boring holidays, years of misapprehension? How do we finally find them—or do they find us, like a happening coming after a dream, which follows the dream's speech and action, so that we say it is our "dream out" . . . It is only infrequently that I now feel that wave of mysterious joy go over me that I once felt in all meetings, partings, chance displays of natural or man-made beauty, accidental losses or gains. . . .

 ⋘   ⋘

SATURDAY 28 AUGUST/65

I am now taking 2 pills in the A.M.—one at 7:30 and one around 10:30. —This morning I thought that the 1st pill was going to see me through; a clear, untroubled interval would show up (take over) every so often—perhaps because I was moving around in the open air, having a *later* breakfast at the restaurant (dump!) and buying things at Sloane's. But soon that secondary sort of *yearning hunger* (which is not real hunger, but is in some way attached to the drug) began again. Heart bumps also slightly involved.

Of course I interpret everything in as black a way as possible. —(My left eye, incidentally, according to the eye man, is holding its own against the vascular difficulty—and the actual sight is not impaired. But, if left to myself, my own diagnosis would have been exceedingly gloomy.)

I *must* get someone to look at my teeth!

And my business affairs must be elucidated. —Some afternoon next week!

A deep-seated masochism? Surely I have acted in a consistently *optimistic* fashion, ever since the 1933 breakdown. —I have surmounted one difficulty after another; I have *worked* for life and "creativity;" I have cast off all the anxieties and fears I could; I have helped others to work and hold on. Why this collapse of psychic energy? Granted that my demands upon both physical and psychic endurance during those last spring weeks in Waltham and Cambridge were clearly excessive—why can't I refuel—recover?

Of course, I must have improved to some degree. My afternoons now (after lunch)—after a (usually) unplanned nap—are nearly normal. The evenings, too—especially after the two drinks I am allowed. —At the moment (11:25) I am hoping to level off after the 2nd pill. Yesterday, I took *three*, in the A.M., including one just after lunch. I nodded off at the eye-doctor's—waiting for him between 12:30 and 1:00. Thereafter I was v. nearly normal, with another pill at supper. (But I was with Ruth from 3:20 on—at a movie.)

How am I going to stand further isolation?

Any *true* writing . . . will have to be done in the *afternoon*. The scraps of stories which I must finally get out of my memory can be attempted in the mornings.

The mere feel of the pen moving across the paper should

be curative. That and *some* attempts to listen to music. —*Who* have I become? *What* has me in hand?

Deliver me!

Let me be strong and free once more.

Or at least *free*—and out of these waves of *malaise*. —For what am I berating myself? What am I afraid of?

Death—for one thing. Yes, that is part of it. —These deaths that are reported in the newspapers seem to be all my age— or younger.

But people keep hopeful and warm and *loving* right to the end—with much more to endure than I endure. —I see the old constantly, on these uptown streets—and they are not "depressed." Their eyes are bright; they have bought themselves groceries; they gossip and laugh—with, often, crippling handicaps evident among them.

Where has this power gone, in my case?

I weep—but there's little relief there.

How can I break these mornings?

Tomorrow I must write another "story." The revelation at Bass Point . . . (But can I tell the whole truth? I never have, even to Dr. Wall. Is the emotional festering begun that far back? —Surely, farther back . . . The early blows somehow *endured* . . .)

LITTLE LOBELIA'S SONG

I was once a part
Of your blood and bone.
Now no longer—
I'm alone, I'm alone.

Each day, at dawn,
I come out of your sleep;
I can't get back.
I weep, I weep.

Not lost but abandoned,
Left behind;
This is my hand
Upon your mind.

I know nothing.
I can barely speak.
But these are my tears
Upon your cheek.

You look at your face
In the looking glass.
This is the face
My likeness has.

Give me back your sleep
Until you die,
Else I weep, weep,
Else I cry, cry.

MONDAY 25 JULY/66

Baddish early on; getting worse around 9–9:45. Typed letters; wrote p.c.s; spoke to Jean and Dr. P. on phone. 2 *Libriums*—close together; then *another* around 9 (?)

Spasms passed around 10:30! Did not return!

TUESDAY 26 JULY
3 pills by 9:30! *Sub* feelings, but no tears. . . .

WEDNESDAY 27 JULY
No tears! 3 pills

THURSDAY 28 JULY
2 early pills (6:30 and 8:30)
Some *tightness* and lowness of spirit, early on. No tears!

15 Back through midnight

🙌 🙌 The north wall contains nothing of interest save the bed and the traveller moored therein, a table, a lamp, and a picture of a water jug, a bowl, two lemons, and a pear (by Vlaminck). The east wall, on the other hand, is filled by an object of immense interest and charm, an object that combines service and beauty in unequal parts. It is an armoire; within its doors lie shirts, towels, pillowcases, and sheets, but the doors themselves—what serviceable quality could dare to compete in importance with this beauty! Vertically, along the edges of the doors, carved from wood, two garlands fall, composed of roses, rose leaves, pine cones, grapes, sunflowers, bursting figs, and lobster claws. The size, the stability of this piece (which has been lent to me by a friend until such time *as she can find a purchaser for it), should hearten the traveller. On the contrary, it is at this point, precisely when the end is in sight, and the starting point almost gained, that the catastrophe of the journey invariably occurs. . . .*

ᘕ ᘕ

Do you have the instructions clear?
    Yes.

Are you ready to answer truthfully?
    Yes.

Do you like to plan alone or with people?
    Alone.

Do you sometimes develop an unreasonable dislike for a person?
    Yes, but it's so slight that I can hide it.

Do you think ordinary people would be shocked if they knew your personal opinions?
    Yes.

When bossy people try to push you around—?
    I do the opposite of what they want.

Does it bother you if people think you're unconventional?
    Not at all.

*If the odds are against something's being a success, would you
still take the risk?*
    Of course.

Do you feel the need to lean on someone in times of sadness?
    Yes.

Can you find energy to face your difficulties?
    Seldom.

"Surprise" is to "strange" as "fear" is to—?
    "Terrible."

LEECHDOMS

Cockayne (T.O.), Editor. Leechdoms, Wortcunning and Starcraft of Early England; Being a Collection of Documents for
the Most Part Never Before Printed, Illustrating the History of
Science in this Country Before the Norman Conquest. Limited
to 500 copies, 3 vols. *buckram, board* £ 16/10/

> Item in Blackwell's catalogue under
> Bibliography, Paleography & Typography

Wortcunning I know;
Starcraft I can find;
But a vision of leechdoms
Has taken hold of my mind.

Where are they found?
Are they forbidden?
Deep in the ground
In a kitchen-midden

With danegelt abandoned?
Crossed by Pict swords?
Mixed up with runes?
Leaking out of word-hoards?

By the salt Saxon sea,
In the blue Druid glade
We shall find leechdoms.
(*Don't be afraid* . . .)

THE CASTLE OF MY HEART

Cleanse and refresh the castle of my heart
Where I have lived for long with little joy.
For Falsest Danger, with its counterpart
Sorrow, has made this siege its long employ.

Now lift the siege, for in your bravest part
Full power exists, most eager for employ;
Cleanse and refresh the castle of my heart
Where I have lived for long with little joy.

Do not let Peril play its lordly part;
Show up the bad game's bait, and its employ.
Nor, for a moment, strut as future's toy.
Advance, and guard your honor and my art.

Cleanse and refresh the castle of my heart.

DECEMBER DAYBREAK

Caught in a corner of the past
Wherein we cannot even weep
We only ask
For present sleep

But the dream shoots forward to a future
We shall never see;
Therefore, in December's night, at the beginning of morning
We must give over, and be

Once again the ignorant victor,
Or the victim, wise
Within those broken circles of wisdom
[   ] which the living live
And the dead rise.

    🖙 🖙

. . . *It is at this point, precisely when the end is in sight, and the starting point almost gained, that the catastrophe of the journey invariably occurs.*

For it is here, as I nearly complete the circle set, that at midnight and in the early morning I encounter the dream. I am set upon by sleep, and hear the rush of water, and hear the mill dam, fuming with water that weighs itself into foam against the air, and see the rapids at its foot that I must gauge and dare and swim. Give over, says this treacherous element, the fear and distress in your breast; and I pretend courage and brave it at last, among rocks along the bank, and plunge into the wave that mounts like glass to the level of my eye. O death, O fear! The universe swings up against my sight, the universe fallen into and bearing with the mill stream. I must in a moment die, but for a moment I breathe, upheld, and see all weight, all force, all water, compacted into the glassy wave, veined, marbled with foam, this moment caught raining over me. And into the wave sinks the armoire, the green bureau, the lamps, the shells from the beach in Maine. All these objects, provisional at best, now equally lost, rock down to translucent depths below fear, an Atlantis in little, under the mill stream (last seen through the steam from the Boston train in March 1909).

First draft written
27 Dec. /07

Copied: 20 January /68

December Daybreak

Caught in a corner of the past
Wherein we cannot even weep
We only ask
For present sleep

But the dream shoots forward to a future
We shall never see,
therefore, in December's night, at the beginning of mourning
We must give over, and be

Once again the ignorant victor,
Or the victim, who
Within those broken girders of wisdom
By which the living live
And the dead pass.

(broken but?)

List
of
Illustrations

Notes
on
Sources

NOTE ON EDITING

Although rigorously selected from their original appearance or
from MS left behind, the texts comprising this book almost always appear exactly as Bogan wrote them. Of the changes that
were made, most are mechanical: adding or dropping punctu-
ation; making two paragraphs where she had one, or one
where she had two. Also under this mechanical umbrella come
the occasional elisions made when I was unable completely to
decipher handwriting or where the focus of a chapter re-
quired them. Usually these elisions are invisible; nearly every
ellipsis is Bogan's own. Having access to both MS and printed
text, I once added a phrase that the printed text had dropped;

no apparatus shows this either. Of a different order of editorial interference is the occasional juggling of the order of paragraphs, sentences, or phrases within a sentence. Whenever this occurs, it is signaled in the Sources by the notation "rearranged." No changes of any kind were made in the poetry.

Abbreviations

Antaeus = "From the Notebooks of Louise Bogan (1935–37)," published posthumously in *Antaeus,* Autumn 1977

APA = *A Poet's Alphabet,* edited by Robert Phelps and Ruth Limmer (New York: McGraw-Hill Book Co., 1970), published posthumously

JAMR = "Journey Around My Room," *The New Yorker,* January 14, 1933

JOAP = "From the Journals of a Poet," published posthumously in *The New Yorker,* January 30, 1978

NYkr = *The New Yorker*

LB Papers = The Louise Bogan Papers at Amherst College. Except as noted, items so labeled have not been previously published.

RL = Ruth Limmer, Louise Bogan's literary executor

TBE = *The Blue Estuaries: Poems 1923–1968* (New York: Farrar, Straus and Giroux, 1968). The reissued Ecco Press edition of 1977 is definitive; it corrects a long-standing typographical error in "Song for the Last Act." Poems not followed with TBE as a final source were also omitted from the *Collected Poems* (New York: Noonday, 1954).

WTWL = *What the Woman Lived: Selected Letters of Louise Bogan, 1920–1970,* edited by Ruth Limmer (New York: Harcourt Brace Jovanovich, 1973), published posthumously

INTRODUCTION

I have very few . . . from letter to Mildred Weston, April 23, 1940

My dislike . . . WTWL, pp. 187–191

Remainder of quotations from conversations with RL, 1959–60

CHRONOLOGY

Except for the 1959 quotation (from letter to Marianne Moore, January 14, 1959, at the Rosenbach Foundation) and the 1966 quotation, as identified, all quotations come from WTWL

CHAPTER 1

Italic passage, JAMR

"Dove and Serpent," NYKR, November 18, 1933

CHAPTER 2

JOAP, passages written June 26, 1953, June 19, 1959, August 27, 1965, June 10, 1957

Italic passage, JAMR

CHAPTER 3

JOAP, passages written January 8, 1954, June 8, 1959

CHAPTER 4

JOAP, written June 22–23, 1959; last paragraph, September 21, 1961

CHAPTER 5

Italic passage, JAMR

"Letdown," NYKR, October 20, 1934. Rearranged.

CHAPTER 6

JOAP, written June 20, 1959, August 16, 1965, September 17, 1960, August 18, 1965

CHAPTER 7

Excerpted from *Partisan Review* symposium, "The Situation in American Writing, 1939," in *The Partisan Reader 1934–44, An Anthology,* edited by William Phillips and Philip Rahv (New York: The Dial Press, 1946), pp. 601–604

Did you ever seek God? LB Papers, November 1930 (?)

"Portrait of the Artist as a Young Woman," LB Papers, 1940 (?)

CHAPTER 8

JOAP, written June 20, 1959

Paragraph on "The Flume," WTWL, p. 8. Rearranged.

"The Flume," *Dark Summer* (New York: Charles Scribner's Sons, 1929)

To make oneself . . . from "The Smith Paper," LB Papers, March 3, 1964

"When at Last," LB Papers, undated

But it's silly . . . on winning the Academy of American Poets Award, quoted to RL, March 1959

"The Engine," NYkr, January 3, 1931

When he sets out . . . from "The Springs of Poetry," *New Republic*, December 5, 1923

"A Letter," *Body of This Death* (New York: R. M. McBride, 1923)

The poet represses . . . JOAP, September 21, 1961

CHAPTER 9

Italic passage, JAMR

Except as noted, the remainder of this chapter comes from the
   LB Papers and was written in 1933

"Coming Out," . . . NYKr, October 14, 1933

"Evening in the Sanitarium," *Nation*, December 10, 1938.
   Originally published with the subtitle "Imitated from
   Auden"

Now I am somewhat better . . . from letter to Janice Biala,
   February 25, 1934, Cornell University Library

CHAPTER 10

The keeping of a journal . . . from preface to *The Journal
   of Jules Renard*, edited and translated by LB and Elizabeth
   Roget (New York: George Braziller, 1964), p. 6

Except as noted, the remainder of this chapter, mostly written
   between 1932 and 1937, comes from Antaeus, JOAP, and
   the LB Papers

"Poem in Prose," *Scribner's Magazine*, January 1935, TBE

"New Moon," *Nation*, August 7, 1937

Dear God . . . letter to RL, April 22, 1961

CHAPTER 11

Although a major achievement . . . excerpted from *America
   Now: an inquiry into civilization in the United States by
   thirty-six Americans*, edited by Harold E. Stearns (New
   York: Charles Scribner's Sons, 1938)

It is difficult to say . . . from a review of Edna St. Vincent
   Millay's *Huntsman, What Quarry?* NYKr, May 20, 1939,
   APA, p. 299

"Kept," *The Sleeping Fury* (New York: Charles Scribner's Sons, 1937) TBE

In the late 30's . . . from *Poet's Choice*, edited by Paul Engle and Joseph Langland (New York: The Dial Press, 1962). Rearranged.

"Zone," *Poems and New Poems* (New York: Charles Scribner's Sons, 1941), TBE

What makes a writer? from a talk at New York University, March 18, 196?, LB Papers

The process by which . . . note accompanying "July Dawn," published as a broadside (San Francisco: Poems in Folio, 1957). Rearranged.

Apprenticeship . . . from a review of Thomas H. Johnson (ed.), *The Poems of Emily Dickinson*, NYkr, October 8, 1955), APA, p. 93

You can think . . . from letter to Mildred Weston, July 9, 1939

Music in those days . . . JOAP, October 16, 1953

"To Be Sung on the Water," NYkr, August 21, 1937, TBE

It is not only pianos . . . Antaeus

My daughter is living with me . . . ; I am a terrible accompanist . . . from letter to Mildred Weston, November 16, 1938

"M. Singing," *Poetry*, December 1936, TBE

I have always found . . . from letter to Morton D. Zabel, June 26, 1937, The Newberry Library, Chicago

The difficulty was . . . JOAP, undated

CHAPTER 12

The strongly poignant . . . JOAP, January 12, 1954

"Packet of Letters," NYkr, January 2, 1937, TBE

I thought that this complex . . . JOAP, ibid.

That year . . . RL's collection, undated

But on the second morning . . . JOAP, ibid.

"To Take Leave," NYkr, January 26, 1935

When it is over . . . JOAP, June 22, 1959

CHAPTER 13

I'm really very proud . . . conversations with RL, 1959–60;
    last sentence from a letter to Glyn Morris, November 26,
    1961

Edmund speaks . . . LB Papers, undated

Dated quotations excerpted from letters and postcards to RL

It is sometimes a good thing . . . "What the Women Said," de-
    livered at Bennington College, October 11, 1962, LB Papers

Your letter . . . adapted from letter to Theodore Roethke,
    November 11, 1962, WTWL, pp. 349–50

CHAPTER 14

All the material in this chapter is drawn from JOAP, with the
    exception of:

I can't believe; In the convent . . . from conversations with
    RL, 1959–60; parenthetical remark from an essay on Rilke,
    written in 1937, APA, p. 354

"The Dragonfly," written September 20–21, 1961, first pub-
    lished in *Poems in Crystal* (New York: The Steuben Glass
    Co., 1963), TBE

It is all based on fact . . . WTWL, p. 332

To trace the dream-landscape . . . ; A perfectly finished
    . . . Antaeus

"Little Lobelia's Song," written October 18 and December
    14, 1966, TBE

CHAPTER 15

Italic passages, JAMR

Do you have the instructions . . . adapted from a question-
naire received by LB in the mail and partially completed in
December 1969; RL's collection

"Leechdoms," written April 21, 1961, draft in LB Papers

"Castle of My Heart," dated February 6, 1966, identified by
Elizabeth Roget as a translation of a rondel by Charles
d'Orléans (1391–1465), LB Papers; excerpted in WTWL,
p. 364

"December Daybreak," first draft written December 27, 1967,
copied January 20, 1968, LB Papers. Against the last three
lines of the poem, LB scribbled a number of question marks.
Among her problems was the first word of the next-to-last
line. LB tried "by" and "through" and was satisfied with
neither. Unlike "Leechdoms," above, for which a holograph
copy exists, "December Daybreak" is still very much unfinished. Readers will, however, understand its inclusion
here.